# BRUSSELS CHRISTMAS TRAVEL GUIDE 2025-2026

## Unwrapping the Spirit of Christmas: A Festive Journeys Through Lights, Winter, Markets, and Tradition

### EMMA JAMES

# Table of Contents

# CHAPTER 1

## WELCOME TO BRUSSELS AT CHRISTMAS!

Every year as December approaches, Brussels takes on a new appearance, making it one of Europe's most appealing holiday destinations. The city comes alive with lights, music, and aromas that permeate its historic streets and squares. From the moment you arrive, you'll notice how the Belgian capital combines its rich history with a welcoming and lively holiday spirit.

The Grand Place, Brussels' central square and a UNESCO World Heritage site, is the focal point of the celebrations. During the holidays, this already stunning square is transformed by a towering Christmas tree and a dazzling sound and light show projected onto the guildhalls' ornate facades. It is a popular gathering place for both locals and visitors, and for many, it is the first and most memorable memory of their trip to the city.

Beyond the Grand Place, the streets of central Brussels are festooned with decorations, holiday markets, and seasonal music. The well known Winter Wonders festival spans several areas, including Place Sainte Catherine and Marché aux

Poisson, forming a trail of market stalls, food stands, and entertainment that invites you to stroll slowly and take it all in. The scent of waffles and mulled wine, the laughter of children skating on the ice rink, or the sight of handcrafted ornaments in wooden chalets all contribute to the holiday atmosphere.

Brussels at Christmas is more than just markets and lights; it also provides an insight into Belgian traditions. Churches hold concerts, neighborhoods illuminate their streets, and families gather for holiday meals. Visitors quickly discover that the holiday season here is both festive and welcoming, with plenty of opportunities to participate.

### 1.1 Introduction: Why is Brussels magical in December?

Brussels in December is unlike any other time of year. The city combines its historic architecture, cobblestone squares, and vibrant culture with the allure of the holiday season, creating an atmosphere that feels warm and festive even in the middle of winter. The air is crisp, the nights arrive early, and the streets are illuminated with thousands of lights, making each walk through the city feel special.

One of the reasons Brussels is so appealing in December is that it celebrates both tradition and creativity. The Grand Place, already one of Europe's most beautiful squares, is transformed into the season's focal point with a towering Christmas tree and a sound and light show. The illuminated façades, set against a backdrop of Gothic and Baroque architecture, create an atmosphere that attracts visitors from all over the world.

The city also comes alive during the Winter Wonders festival, which spans several squares and streets. More than just a Christmas market, it offers a complete holiday experience with food stands, craft stalls, concerts, ice skating, and even a Ferris wheel with panoramic views of Brussels' lights. This combination of sights, tastes, and activities keeps the city feeling alive throughout December.

Belgians enjoy seasonal flavors, which contribute to this atmosphere. Whether it's hot chocolate rich enough to warm you after a long walk, spiced speculoos biscuits tied to Saint Nicholas traditions, or a festive beer brewed just for the holiday season, December's culinary delights are a big part of why visitors enjoy Brussels during this time of year.

Brussels also exudes a welcoming spirit that makes visitors feel included in its festivities. While Brussels is Europe's capital with a very international character, December feels personal, with both locals and tourists sharing the same squares, markets, and winter activities. This combination of grand events and simple pleasures distinguishes the city's December atmosphere.

## 1.2 How Brussels changes during the holiday season

Brussels in December is almost unrecognizable from the rest of the year. The city's streets, squares, and landmarks are festooned with lights, greenery, and decorations, transforming the Belgian capital into a massive open-air celebration. What was once a bustling European hub of politics, business, and daily life is transformed into a place where people slow down, stroll through illuminated alleys, and gather in markets to celebrate the season.

The most striking transformation occurs in the Grand Place. By day, its historic guildhalls make it one of Europe's most beautiful squares, but come December, it transforms into a true holiday stage. A massive Christmas tree towers in the center, often reaching more than 20 meters tall and adorned with sparkling lights and ornaments. Each evening, the square's façades come to life with a sound and light show that combines music, colors, and animation to cast a magical glow over the entire square.

The festive spirit spreads beyond the Grand Place. Boulevard Anspach and the lanes leading to Place Sainte Catherine are lit up for the holidays, and wooden chalets sell everything from ornaments to seasonal treats. This is the heart of Winter Wonders, Brussels' main Christmas celebration. It spans a large area and features an ice rink, a Ferris wheel, and rows of market stalls, creating a winter village atmosphere in the heart of the city.

Public spaces throughout Brussels are also participating in the transformation. The Bourse building and Place de la Monnaie are adorned with imaginative light installations. Neighborhoods and shopping streets, such as Avenue Louise and Rue Neuve, set up their own displays to attract shoppers looking for Christmas presents. Even smaller squares, like Place du Marché aux Poisson, have themed decorations and food vendors, contributing to the citywide celebration.

Cultural venues also help to create a festive atmosphere. Seasonal performances in concert halls, theaters, and churches include classical music, choirs, and Christmas plays. Museums extend their hours or host holiday themed activities, while restaurants and cafés decorate their interiors to provide a cozy setting for people to enjoy Belgian hot chocolate, mulled wine, or hearty winter dishes.

Brussels' holiday season is more than just decoration; it is a shift in the city's rhythm. Everyday life blends with celebration, and both visitors and residents enjoy the atmosphere. What makes the transformation so memorable is that it spreads throughout the city, making December in Brussels a truly festive experience.

# CHAPTER 2

## BRUSSELS IN THE HOLIDAY SPIRIT

When December arrives, Brussels emits a warmth that contrasts nicely with the cool winter air. The city embraces the holiday season with a grand and welcoming personality, giving visitors an immediate sense of being a part of the festivities. Walking through the streets, you'll notice glowing arches stretched over shopping avenues, windows adorned with wreaths and garlands, and squares transformed into lively gathering places full of music and laughter.

The Grand Place is the center of this spirit. Each evening, a light and sound show illuminates the historic square, attracting crowds who stop to watch the colors dance across the ornate façades. The Winter Wonders festival, located just a short walk away, spreads throughout the city center, with families, couples, and friends moving between chalets offering crafts, sweets, and steaming drinks.

The scent of roasted chestnuts and mulled wine permeates the air, while carousels, ice skating, and the Ferris wheel create the atmosphere of a holiday fair.

Beyond the main festival areas, the holiday spirit permeates every part of Brussels. Churches hold seasonal concerts, local bakeries stock their shelves with festive treats, and neighborhoods decorate themselves, all of which contribute to a strong sense of community that visitors notice. The city transforms into a hub for both traditional and modern celebrations, allowing everyone to share in the joy of the season.

## 2.1 Overview of Festive Neighborhoods

Several neighborhoods in Brussels play an important role in the city's holiday atmosphere, each adding its own flavor to the festivities.

The Grand Place and its surrounding streets are the hub of the festivities. With its towering Christmas tree, glowing decorations, and nightly light shows, the square is the city's most popular gathering place in December. Just beyond, the narrow lanes of the historic center are lined with shops, cafés, and market stalls that keep the festive spirit alive.

Moving toward Place Sainte Catherine and the Marché aux Poissons, you'll find one of the Winter Wonders festival's largest areas. Wooden chalets line the square, selling crafts, food, and drinks, while the Ferris wheel and merry go round add a playful element that appeals to both children and adults. This part of the city resembles a winter village set against the backdrop of Brussels' historic streets. Seasonal lights and performances on Boulevard Anspach and nearby squares such as Place de la Monnaie add to the buzz. Shoppers and visitors come here to enjoy music, street entertainment, and the decorated facades of historic buildings.

Avenue Louise provides a more elegant perspective on the holidays for those looking for something different. The avenue is known for its high end boutiques and is beautifully illuminated, making it a popular spot for evening strolls and holiday shopping.

These neighborhoods work together to form a network of celebrations that spans central Brussels, ensuring that wherever you go in December, you are surrounded by the season's sights, sounds, and flavors.

## 2.2 The Grand Place's light displays and Christmas tree

The Grand Place is the focal point of Brussels' Christmas season and one of Europe's most iconic holiday destinations. The square, which is already well known throughout the year for its ornate guildhalls, Town Hall, and King's House (Maison du Roi), takes on a completely different personality in December. Its transformation revolves around two main features: the magnificent Christmas tree and the evening light shows, which transform the square into a living spectacle.

The Christmas tree, placed in the heart of the square, is more than just a decoration; it is a tradition that attracts visitors from all over the world. Every year, a tree, usually a spruce, is carefully selected and donated from the Ardennes region of Belgium or neighboring countries. It towers over the cobblestones, often more than 20 meters tall, and is adorned with strings of glowing lights, shimmering ornaments, and a large star at the top. The tree's size and beauty make it the focal point of the square, and it's nearly impossible to walk through the city center in December without stopping to admire it.

The Grand Place's famous sound and light show begins each evening, adding to its enchanting atmosphere. The show, which is projected onto the facades of the square's historic buildings, combines music and carefully choreographed lighting effects. The intricate details of the Gothic Town Hall and the Baroque guildhalls are highlighted by colors that shift and pulse in time with festive tunes ranging from classical carols to modern holiday music. The shows are free and run several times throughout the evening, allowing both locals and visitors to enjoy the experience without purchasing a ticket.

The atmosphere at these performances is unlike anything else in Brussels. Crowds gather in the square, bundled in scarves and gloves, holding cups of hot chocolate or mulled wine and watching the buildings come to life. The massive tree, lights, and music create a setting that is both grand and intimate, transforming the Grand Place into the hub of the city's holiday festivities.

The Christmas tree and light shows are more than just visual spectacles; they capture the essence of Brussels in December. They bring together locals, visitors, families, and friends in one of the city's most historic spaces to share in a moment of wonder. For many visitors, this is the highlight of their Christmas vacation, a memory that lasts long after the season is over.

The beauty of Brussels at Christmas extends far beyond the Grande Place. The entire city center joins in the celebration, transforming ordinary streets and squares into glowing winter scenes. Seasonal decorations are carefully arranged to highlight the city's historic architecture while also creating a warm, festive atmosphere that draws visitors deeper into the neighborhoods.

Walking from the Grand Place to Place Sainte Catherine, strings of sparkling lights drape across narrow streets, creating illuminated tunnels that lead to the Winter Wonders festival area. The chalets and food stands are decorated with garlands, pine branches, and ornaments, and the Ferris wheel is illuminated with thousands of bulbs, becoming a Christmas landmark in the city. The nearby Marché aux Poissons is also a popular destination, where holiday decorations blend with the lively energy of families and friends enjoying seasonal food and beverages.

The Bourse building, located on Boulevard Anspach, is another notable landmark. Its neoclassical façade is frequently lit with vibrant colors and creative light installations that change with the seasons, making it a popular photo location. Place de la Monnaie, a short walk away, is also beautifully illuminated, with lights reflecting off the opera house and festive stalls scattered throughout the square.

Shopping streets develop their own distinct festive style. Rue Neuve, Brussels' busiest shopping street, is decorated with glowing arches that form a canopy of lights for holiday shoppers. The more upscale Avenue Louise, known for luxury boutiques, features elegant displays that combine twinkling white lights with refined decorations, making evening walks here particularly atmospheric. Smaller side streets and squares, such as Place du Grand Sablon, enhance the atmosphere with tasteful lighting and Christmas trees surrounded by antique shops and chocolatiers.

Brussels' decorations extend beyond its streets and squares. Restaurants and cafés participate in the celebration by decorating their windows with wreaths, twinkling lights, and small fir trees placed at the entrances. Department stores and boutiques create elaborate window displays that combine creativity and holiday traditions, frequently featuring chocolate sculptures, winter scenes, or handcrafted ornaments. Even public transportation hubs such as Gare Centrale and Gare du Midi have seasonal touches, reminding visitors that the holiday spirit extends throughout the city.

What distinguishes Brussels' seasonal decorations is the way they connect to form a continuous holiday trail. From grand squares to hidden alleys, the entire city feels involved in the celebration, encouraging visitors to venture beyond the main attractions. The result is an immersive environment in which each turn reveals something new, whether it's a glowing façade, a decorated street, or a warmly lit café inviting you inside.

# CHAPTER 3

## WINTER WONDERS AND CHRISTMAS MARKET EXPERIENCE

The Winter Wonders festival is the highlight of Brussels' holiday season and one of the most popular Christmas events in Europe. It lasts several weeks, from late November to early January, and transforms the city center into a vibrant winter village complete with lights, music, and seasonal flavors. The festival encompasses key areas such as Place Sainte Catherine, the Marché aux Poissons, and the streets that connect them to the Grand Place, forming a festive trail that is easily explored on foot.

More than 200 wooden chalets selling a variety of goods serve as the focal point of the experience. Visitors can browse handmade ornaments, wool clothing, jewelry, and traditional crafts, making it an ideal location for finding unique gifts. Along with the crafts, there are food stalls selling Belgian specialties like waffles, fries, and speculoos, as well as international favorites like raclette, sausages, and mulled wine. The aromas of roasting chestnuts and hot drinks permeate the air, enticing visitors to stay and try different treats.

The market is also intended for entertainment. Every year, an ice skating rink is set up, attracting families, couples, and groups of friends to glide across the ice, which is illuminated with festive lights. A Ferris wheel near Place Sainte Catherine provides panoramic views of the decorated city, especially at night when the streets below glow with color. Carousels, light installations, and live performances create a lively atmosphere suitable for people of all ages.

What distinguishes Winter Wonders is the way it combines traditional Christmas market charm with large scale festive events. It's more than just shopping and eating; it's about being a part of a celebration that infuses the city center with joy and energy. The combination of historic squares, seasonal decorations, and holiday activities makes every visit to the market memorable, whether you spend an hour wandering or an entire evening immersed in the atmosphere.

### 3.1 History and Significance of Brussels' Winter Wonders

The Winter Wonders festival has become one of Brussels' defining holiday traditions, despite its relatively recent history in comparison to neighboring Germany and France's century old

Christmas markets. The festival was officially launched in 2000 as a way to combine Brussels' existing Christmas market and a growing calendar of seasonal events into a single cohesive celebration. Since then, it has grown to become one of Europe's most well known winter festivals, attracting more than 2.5 million visitors annually.

Winter Wonders was originally intended to be more than just a marketplace. The city wanted to organize an event that reflected Brussels' multicultural identity and international outlook. This vision shaped the event's character: rather than focusing solely on Belgian traditions, Winter Wonders included international cuisine, global crafts, and cultural performances, making the festival representative of the city's diverse communities. At the same time, it has always valued Belgian heritage, emphasizing local specialties such as speculoos biscuits, mulled wine, artisanal chocolate, and the comfort of traditional wooden chalets.

The decision to hold the festival near Place Sainte Catherine and the Marché aux Poissons gave it an immediate appeal. These historical and architecturally significant areas served as an authentic backdrop, balancing an old world atmosphere with modern festive installations. Over the years, the event has spread from the Grand Place, with its famous light and sound show, to boulevards, squares, and shopping streets, ensuring that the entire city center participates in the festivities.

Winter Wonders has also gained prominence for its contribution to Brussels' cultural and economic life. It provides a significant boost to local businesses ranging from chocolatiers and restaurants to hotels and boutique stores. The festival has grown into an attraction that puts Brussels on the map alongside other well known European Christmas destinations such as Vienna, Strasbourg, and Köln.

Equally important is the festival's role in fostering a sense of community. It is popular with both tourists and locals, who return year after year to skate at the rink, meet friends at the market stalls, and admire the lights with their families. For many locals, it marks the true start of the festive season in Brussels, a tradition that has become inextricably linked to city life.

Winter Wonders has grown from a holiday initiative to a symbol of Brussels' holiday spirit in just over two decades, combining tradition, modern creativity, and international flair. Its history demonstrates how a relatively new event can evolve into something treasured by both the city's residents and the millions who travel from all over the world to participate.

The layout of Brussels' Winter Wonders and Christmas Market is one of the elements that make it both visually appealing and easy to navigate. The market is not confined to a single square, but rather spread across several of the city's most iconic locations, forming a festive corridor that runs from the Grand Place down winding streets to Place Sainte Catherine and the Marché aux Poissons. This layout encourages visitors to walk, explore, and enjoy the holiday atmosphere at their leisure, while encountering various themes and attractions along the way.

The journey often starts at the Grand Place, Brussels' central square, and a UNESCO World Heritage Site. Visitors are greeted by the towering Christmas tree, the nativity scene, and the captivating light and sound show that illuminates the historic guildhalls and Town Hall. Although the Grand Place does not have market stalls, it sets the tone with its stunning display and serves as the symbolic entrance to the Winter Wonders trail.

The festive path leads from the Grand Place through nearby streets such as Rue de la Bourse and Boulevard Anspach to the Bourse building. During the season, the former Brussels Stock Exchange is illuminated with colorful lights, and its steps are frequently used as a gathering point before entering the market's heart. The streets leading away from here are lined with decorated stalls selling crafts, food, and gifts, providing the first glimpse of the market atmosphere.

The trail continues to Place de la Monnaie, where smaller clusters of stalls and performances provide variety. This square frequently hosts live music or artistic light displays, beckoning visitors to pause before continuing on. From there, the festive path broadens into the main market areas, Place Sainte Catherine and Marché aux Poissons.

The former church square at Place Sainte Catherine has been transformed into one of Winter Wonders' main attractions. Wooden chalets selling holiday goods surround the church, and food stalls entice visitors with sweet and savory treats. This square is also a popular spot for people to enjoy mulled wine or Belgian waffles under the Christmas lights.

Just behind Place Sainte Catherine is the Marché aux Poissons, a historic former fish market that has been transformed into the Winter Wonders festival's largest and most vibrant section. Dozens of chalets line the long rectangular square, selling everything from handmade gifts to steaming dishes from all over the world. The atmosphere is enhanced by the Ferris wheel, which towers above the market and offers panoramic views of the city lit up for the season. This area also has an ice skating rink, which is surrounded by festive lights and music, making it a popular spot for families and groups of friends.

This linear but connected layout, which begins with the grandeur of the Grand Place and ends with the vibrant energy of Vismet, creates a natural flow that visitors can follow without the use of maps. Every corner offers something unique, from light installations and performances to food tastings and artisanal shopping. The market's design ensures that no single space feels overcrowded, and each section has its own identity, resulting in a diverse but seamless experience.

### 3.3 Must see chalets and artisan stalls

Wandering among the wooden chalets, each of which is illuminated and filled with treasures ranging from edible delights to handmade crafts, is one of the highlights of the Brussels Winter Wonders Market. While there are over 200 stalls to explore, a few stand out as truly memorable stops for visitors looking for a combination of tradition, quality, and local flavor.

The Belgian chocolate stalls are the focal point of the experience. Artisans like Passion Chocolate and smaller independent chocolatiers frequently set up chalets on Place Sainte Catherine to sell pralines, truffles, and hot chocolate that highlight the city's world renowned craft. These stalls are great for picking up indulgent treats and beautifully packaged gifts.

The speculoos biscuit vendors are also appealing, offering freshly baked cookies flavored with cinnamon and spices. Some stalls even sell decorative tins filled with speculoos that are convenient to transport home. Nearby, there are often stands selling cube dons, a traditional Belgian sweet shaped like a cone and filled with syrupy fruit flavors.

For savory options, the market chalets serve both Belgian classics and international cuisine. Visitors to the Marché aux Poissons will find stands selling raclette, which is melted cheese scraped onto bread or potatoes, as well as steaming tartiflette, sausages, and dishes from around Europe. Belgian specialties such as stoemp (mashed potatoes with vegetables) and carbonnade (Flemish beef stew) are also served at some food chalets, providing a taste of hearty winter comfort food.

Shoppers looking for crafts will find plenty of artisan stalls to visit. Among the most popular are the hand blown glass ornament makers, whose delicate baubles sparkle under the market lights, and the woodcarvers, who sell toys, nativity figures, and small home decor. Hand knit scarves, wool hats, and mittens made by local artisans are also useful and attractive souvenirs.

Aside from Belgian goods, Winter Wonders has an international flair. Some chalets feature handcrafted items from other countries, such as Alpine-style decorations from Austria and Switzerland or Eastern European textiles. This blend of local and global craftsmanship reflects Brussels' cosmopolitan spirit and ensures that each visitor discovers something unique.

For those who enjoy browsing unusual finds, look for stalls selling candleholders carved from natural wood, artisan soaps scented with winter spices, and hand-poured beeswax candles. These smaller crafts are often made by family businesses, adding a personal touch to the shopping experience.

The diversity of the chalets is what makes them so appealing. No two stalls are alike, and even a leisurely stroll from Place Sainte Catherine to Vismet reveals dozens of discoveries to be made. The must see chalets, whether selling warm chocolate, glowing ornaments, or hand knit woolens, are more than just shops; they are part of the story of Brussels at Christmas, where local tradition and seasonal spirit intersect in every corner of the market.

### 3.4 Special activities: ice skating, Ferris wheel, and light parades

Brussels' Winter Wonders is more than just a Christmas market; it's an immersive festival full of holiday themed activities. While browsing chalets and sampling seasonal foods is enjoyable, the event's unique attractions allow visitors to experience the city in magical and memorable ways. The ice skating rink, the Ferris wheel, and the light parades are three of the most iconic attractions, each adding their own unique charm to the holiday season.

One of the main attractions at Winter Wonders is the ice skating rink, which is located in the lively Marché aux Poissons area. Surrounded by glowing chalets, festive music, and seasonal decorations, the rink provides a winter playground for people of all ages. Families gather in the afternoons to watch children make their first glides on the ice, while couples and groups of friends skate under the evening lights. Skates are available for rent, and the rink is designed to accommodate both novice and experienced skaters, making it one of the most inclusive and enjoyable activities at the festival. Warm drinks and snacks sold nearby are an excellent way to unwind after a day on the ice.

The Ferris wheel, another Winter Wonders landmark, towers above the market. Its illuminated structure, visible from all over the city center, makes it impossible to miss. A ride on the Ferris wheel provides panoramic views of Brussels, with the rooftops, church towers, and streets below illuminated by holiday lights. The Grand Place, Sainte Catherine, and the long rows of chalets sparkle against the winter sky, making for a particularly breathtaking view at night. For many visitors, this ride is one of the most memorable parts of their Christmas vacation, combining a sense of fun with the beauty of the city's holiday transformation.

The light parades, which take place on select evenings throughout December, add a lively, artistic element to the festival. These processions pass through the city center's decorated streets, carrying illuminated floats, costumed performers, and musicians. The parades add excitement and surprise, filling the air with festive music and vibrant colors. Children are frequently captivated by the vibrant costumes and playful characters, while adults value the artistry and creativity that distinguishes each parade. The routes usually pass through the central squares, ensuring that visitors to the market can easily see the spectacle.

Together, these activities take Winter Wonders beyond the typical Christmas market setting. The ice skating rink encourages participation, the Ferris wheel provides perspective and wonder, and the light parades add a theatrical element to the streets. Each is intended not only to entertain but also to create long lasting memories, transforming a stroll through Brussels in December into a full holiday experience.

# CHAPTER 4

## BELGIAN HOLIDAY FOOD AND DRINK

A visit to Brussels at Christmas is incomplete without sampling the seasonal foods and beverages that fill the market stalls with warmth and aroma. Belgian classics take center stage, providing warmth against the winter chill. Freshly baked waffles, dusted with sugar or topped with chocolate, are popular choices for anyone visiting the market. Stalls selling frites with rich sauces remind visitors of the country's culinary heritage, while steaming bowls of carbonnade flamande (Flemish beef stew) or stoemp (mashed potatoes with vegetables) add hearty flavors to the season.

For sweet treats, the festive stalls are brimming with speculoos biscuits, gingerbread, and pralines from Brussels' master chocolatiers. Seasonal drinks, such as vin chaud (mulled wine) and hot chocolate, are served from steaming pots, filling the air with cinnamon, clove, and cocoa aromas. Belgian beers, which are frequently brewed in limited edition Christmas styles, offer another way to feel the holiday spirit. Together, these dishes and drinks create a food experience that combines local tradition with festive indulgence, making the market both a culinary journey and a visual celebration.

## 4.1 Traditional Belgian Christmas dishes: turkey, game, and festive feasts

Christmas in Belgium is as much about getting together around the table as it is about festive decorations and markets. Holiday meals are an important part of the celebration, often prepared with care and enjoyed with family and friends in a warm, cozy setting. While there are regional variations throughout the country, a few dishes consistently appear on Christmas menus, reflecting both Belgian tradition and the season's spirit of indulgence.

Roast turkey is the centerpiece of many Belgian Christmas feasts, often stuffed with herbs, vegetables, and dried fruits or chestnuts. Turkey gained popularity as a festive centerpiece in the twentieth century, and in Belgium, it is typically served with roasted potatoes, seasonal vegetables such as Brussels sprouts, and a rich gravy or cranberry sauce. In some households, goose or capon may be served instead, but turkey remains the most popular option.

Game dishes are another staple of Belgian Christmas dinners, especially in rural areas or among families that value traditional recipes. Venison, wild boar, pheasant, and duck are frequently served on holiday tables, prepared with robust flavors appropriate for the winter season. These dishes are frequently slow cooked or roasted and served with sauces made of red wine, juniper berries, or mushrooms. Winter vegetables and potato gratins are common side dishes, helping to balance the game's strong flavors with comforting accompaniments.

Beyond the main course, Christmas in Belgium includes elaborate starters and desserts. Many meals start with foie gras, smoked salmon, or seafood platters, reflecting Belgium's proximity to the North Sea and culinary preference for fresh, high quality produce. Oysters are a popular holiday delicacy, usually served with sparkling wine or Champagne.

Desserts are where Belgian ingenuity shines. Families may prepare a bûche de Noël (Yule log cake), decorated to resemble a snowy log, or serve cougnou, a sweet bread shaped like the baby Jesus, a tradition particularly strong in Wallonia. Belgian pralines and truffles, as well as speculoos biscuits and gingerbread, are common holiday treats.

Festive beverages are equally important. A Belgian Christmas feast can be paired with fine wines, Champagne, or specialty Christmas beers brewed by local breweries. These beers, which are often spiced and stronger than regular varieties, complement the rich flavors of holiday dishes and are highly anticipated each year.

These traditional Belgian Christmas dishes demonstrate the country's preference for seasonal, hearty, and meticulously prepared meals. Whether it's a golden roast turkey, a richly flavored game dish, or a beautifully decorated Yule log, the food serves as both sustenance and a symbol of togetherness, defining the holiday as one of warmth, generosity, and shared celebration.

## *4.2 Street food delights include waffles, fries, and roasted chestnuts*

The festive streets of Brussels in December are filled with the irresistible aromas of warm, comforting street food. These seasonal favorites serve not only as quick snacks, but also contribute significantly to the city's Christmas atmosphere. Visitors strolling through the Winter Wonders market frequently stop at chalets and street stands to sample these Belgian classics, which have become traditions in their own right.

## *Waffles*

Waffles are perhaps the most well known Belgian street food, and they are especially popular during the holidays. There are two main types: the lighter, rectangular Brussels waffle, which is crisp on the outside and soft on the inside, and the smaller, denser Liège waffle, which is sweetened with chunks of pearl sugar that caramelize while cooking. Waffles at the Christmas market are typically served hot from the iron, dusted with powdered sugar, and topped with whipped cream, chocolate sauce, fruit, or speculoos spread. Eating one while strolling through the decorated squares is an experience that combines flavor and atmosphere, making waffles a must try during any winter visit.

## *Fries*

Belgian fries, also known as frites, are a popular snack, especially on cold evenings. Unlike regular fries, they are cut thick and fried twice, giving them a crisp golden exterior and fluffy interior. Street vendors at the Winter Wonders market serve fries in iconic paper cones, frequently accompanied by a generous helping of mayonnaise or one of the many Belgian sauces, such as andalouse (a tangy tomato and pepper sauce) or samurai (a spicy mayonnaise blend). The sight of visitors strolling the festive streets with steaming cones of fries in hand is as much a part of the holiday atmosphere as the lights and music.

### Roasted chestnuts

Roasted chestnuts add a traditional and nostalgic flavor to the holiday season. Vendors roast them over open flames in small carts, filling the air with a smoky, nutty aroma that immediately transports you to the warmth of winter. Served in simple paper cones, the chestnuts are soft, slightly sweet, and ideal for warming cold hands while exploring the market. Their presence gives the festivities a timeless charm, reminding visitors of centuries-old Christmas traditions.

Waffles, fries, and roasted chestnuts embody the essence of Brussels' holiday street food: simple, satisfying, and rich in tradition. They are more than just snacks; they are part of the sensory experience that makes walking around the city in December so enjoyable. Each bite embodies some of the warmth and comfort that define Christmas in Belgium.

Belgium's sweet traditions shine brightest during the holiday season, when markets, chocolatiers, and bakeries stock their shelves with treats that are both beautiful and delicious. Among the most popular are pralines, speculoos, and marzipan, each with its own story and seasonal appeal. These sweets are more than just indulgences; they are part of the holiday tradition, frequently exchanged as gifts or enjoyed at family gatherings.

### *Pralines*

Belgium is well known for its pralines, which are delicate chocolate shells filled with ganache, cream, caramel, or nut paste. Pralines were first created in Brussels in 1912 by chocolatier Jean Neuhaus and have since become a symbol of Belgian craftsmanship. During the holidays, chocolatiers such as Neuhaus, Godiva, and Leonidas release special holiday collections in festive boxes, making them popular gift options. Walking through the Winter Wonders market, visitors will notice smaller artisan stalls selling pralines made by local chocolatiers, which are often decorated with seasonal touches such as gold dust, snowflake designs, or flavors inspired by holiday spices.

## Speculoos

Speculoos biscuits are another Belgian holiday tradition. These spiced cookies, flavored with cinnamon, nutmeg, cloves, and brown sugar, are baked into flat, rectangular shapes that may bear festive imprints. Traditionally eaten on Saint Nicholas Day (December 6), they are still popular throughout the Christmas season. Many market stalls sell them freshly baked, while others sell jars of speculoos spread, a creamy version of the biscuit that has gained popularity far beyond Belgium. Visitors can also find speculoos used creatively, such as crumbling it over hot chocolate, layering it into desserts, or pairing it with pralines for a double dose of Belgian sweetness.

## Marzipan

Marzipan plays an important role in Belgian holiday traditions, particularly in Brussels, where it is sold in charming pastel colored blocks and sculpted into festive shapes. Marzipan, made from almonds and sugar, is chewy and sweet, with a rich nutty flavor. Around Christmas, shops display marzipan molded into miniature fruits, animals, or holiday figures, which are both visually appealing and delicious. Marzipan is associated with Saint Nicholas in some parts of Belgium, but it is widely available and enjoyed as a seasonal treat at Christmas markets.

Pralines, speculoos, and marzipan show off the variety and creativity of Belgian sweets. Each one represents a different aspect of the country's culinary heritage: pralines highlight chocolate innovation, speculoos connect to long standing festive traditions, and marzipan adds a playful, decorative touch to holiday displays. For visitors, sampling these treats means not only enjoying the flavors, but also participating in the timeless traditions that make a Belgian Christmas so special.

### 4.4 Festive beverages include Belgian Christmas beers, mulled wine, and hot chocolate

No holiday in Brussels is complete without trying the festive drinks that warm the season and bring people together. From traditional spiced wines to Belgium's world famous beers and rich chocolates, these drinks are more than just refreshments; they are an integral part of the city's Christmas spirit.

### Belgian Christmas beers

Belgium's brewing heritage is legendary, and it takes on a special meaning around Christmas. Many breweries create seasonal beers that are stronger, darker, and spiced to reflect the winter season. Popular varieties include St. Bernardus Christmas Ale, which has caramel and dried fruit notes, as well as Delirium Christmas, which has a festive label and a full bodied flavor. Around the holidays, some Trappist breweries release limited editions, which are often spiced with cinnamon, cloves, or nutmeg. These beers are served in chalets at the Winter Wonders market and cozy cafés throughout the city, making them a must try for visitors looking to experience Belgian tradition.

### Mulled wine (Vin Chaud or Glühwein)

Mulled wine is one of the most iconic drinks at the Brussels Christmas market. Vin chaud, or glühwein in Dutch, is made by slowly warming red wine with cinnamon, star anise, cloves, and citrus. Vendors serve it hot in festive cups, and the sweet, spiced aroma permeates the market squares. Sipping mulled wine while strolling between chalets or watching the Grand Place light show has become a popular tradition among both locals and visitors. Some stalls also serve variations, such as white mulled wine or versions infused with brandy or rum for an added kick.

### Hot Chocolate

Because of Belgium's reputation for producing fine chocolate, hot chocolate is a natural holiday favorite. Hot chocolate is served thick, creamy, and indulgent at the Winter Wonders market and in renowned cafés such as Maison Dandoy and Pierre Marcolini. It is often made with real melted Belgian chocolate rather than cocoa powder and is rich enough to serve as a dessert on its own. Toppings like whipped cream, marshmallows, and speculoos crumbs enhance the festive atmosphere. For many families, warming up with hot chocolate after skating or shopping is one of the season's most comforting traditions.

Belgian Christmas beers, mulled wine, and hot chocolate make up the trio of holiday beverages that define Brussels in December. Each reflects a different aspect of the celebration: beer honors Belgium's heritage, mulled wine evokes the timeless flavors of European Christmas markets, and hot chocolate is pure indulgence. When enjoyed under the glow of festive lights, they bring warmth and cheer to every moment of the holiday season.

# CHAPTER 5

## BRUSSELS BY DAY AND NIGHT

Visiting Brussels at Christmas means seeing the city in two very different but equally enchanting light displays. By day, the city's historic architecture, cobblestone streets, and bustling squares come alive with market activity. Visitors can wander through the chalets on Place Sainte Catherine or admire the details of the Grand Place's ornate architecture. Cafés are bustling with hot drinks, museums welcome visitors seeking art and history, and festive decorations stand out against the winter sunlight. Daytime is ideal for taking a stroll through neighborhoods, shopping for gifts, and sampling holiday treats outside.

At night, Brussels transforms into something truly magical. The city is illuminated by thousands of lights, with illuminated streets leading to the shimmering heart of the Grand Place. The evening sound and light show illuminates the square, while the Ferris wheel and ice rink at Vismet sparkle against the night sky. Walking through the market in the evening creates a completely different atmosphere, with mulled wine in hand, live performances, and music adding to the festive spirit. Day and night experiences work together to create a balance between discovery and detail during the day and wonder and celebration at night.

During the holiday season, daytime in Brussels invites you to take your time and discover the city's charm. The soft winter sunlight accentuates the details of historic façades, and the festive atmosphere makes walking tours especially enjoyable. Visitors can combine the excitement of the markets with cultural discoveries, resulting in an experience that combines tradition, history, and seasonal spirit.

The Grand Place is an excellent starting point for any daytime tour, as the magnificent guildhalls and Town Hall are more visible in daylight. From here, guided walking tours frequently take you through the winding streets of Brussels' historic heart, the Îlot Sacré, which is lined with old taverns, chocolate shops, and welcoming cafés. Cultural walks during the holidays frequently include stops at local chocolatiers or bakeries, where visitors can sample pralines, speculoos, and other festive sweets while learning about the city's culinary traditions.

Another popular festive walk leads to the Galeries Royales Saint Hubert, a 19th century glass roofed shopping arcade. The galleries, which are decked out in Christmas garlands and lights, make for a lovely daytime stop, with luxury boutiques, theaters, and cafés that glow with holiday displays. The nearby Place du Grand Sablon adds an elegant touch to any tour, particularly for those interested in antiques, art galleries, and fine chocolate.

For those looking for a more seasonal focus, daytime festive tours frequently visit the Winter Wonders areas around Place Sainte Catherine and the Marché aux Poissons. By day, these squares are less crowded than in the evenings, making it easier to browse artisan stalls, shop for crafts, or simply enjoy the festive scenery at a slower pace. Street performers and musicians occasionally appear in these areas in the afternoons, adding to the lively atmosphere.

Cultural walks also include visits to major landmarks in Brussels, such as the Cathedral of St. Michael and St. Gudula, whose Gothic towers rise dramatically above the city. During December, the cathedral frequently hosts nativity displays and special concerts that complement a daytime cultural itinerary. Visitors interested in history and art can also visit nearby museums, such as the

Magritte Museum or the Museum of the City of Brussels, to add depth to their day's explorations.

Daytime festive tours and cultural walks are more than just sightseeing; they provide an opportunity to immerse oneself in the rhythms of the city. The combination of open air markets, historic landmarks, and seasonal stops strikes a balance between discovery and celebration. With the crisp winter air and the sound of carols floating from market squares, exploring Brussels by day feels like entering a story where culture and Christmas traditions intersect at every turn.

## 5.2 Nightlife at Christmas: bars, pubs, and Christmas concerts

When evening falls, Brussels takes on a different kind of magic, as the festive atmosphere shifts from the bustling markets to the vibrant nightlife. The city's bars, pubs, and music venues are filled with holiday spirit, making the nights in December just as enjoyable as the days. Visitors looking to experience Brussels after dark have a variety of options, ranging from cozy drinking spots to grand halls filled with seasonal music.

### Bars & Pubs

Brussels is well known for its beer culture, and December is an ideal time to explore it. Traditional pubs like À La Mort Subite (7 Rue Montagne aux Herbes Potagères, 1000 Brussels) and Delirium Café (Impasse de la Fidélité 4, 1000 Brussels) offer seasonal Belgian Christmas beers and year round classics. These beers are typically darker, spicier, and richer, brewed specifically for the winter months. Smaller neighborhood bars also celebrate the holiday season by decorating with lights and serving mulled wine or hot cocktails to warm guests after a cold evening walk.

### Christmas Concerts and Performances

The holiday nights in Brussels revolve around music. The Cathedral of St. Michael and St. Gudula frequently hosts classical Christmas concerts, which fill the Gothic interior with carols, choirs, and organ music. Visitors to the Palais des Beaux Arts (BOZAR) can enjoy seasonal symphonies, jazz performances, and special holiday programs. Smaller venues, such as local churches and community halls, also host free or low cost concerts, providing visitors with a more intimate experience of Belgian traditions. These concerts are typically focused on choral singing or instrumental music, creating a warm and reflective atmosphere amidst the holiday frenzy.

## Seasonal Entertainment

Beyond traditional pubs and concerts, Brussels has a festive nightlife with a playful twist. The Winter Wonders area remains open late, with the Ferris wheel and ice rink illuminated against the night sky. Many stalls continue to serve hot drinks and snacks late into the evening, turning the market into a social hub. The bars around Place Sainte Catherine and Bourse are packed with locals and tourists, with heated and decorated terraces that create a lively atmosphere.

For those who enjoy late night energy, some venues in Saint Géry or the Louise district incorporate holiday themes into their nightlife, hosting Christmas themed parties or DJ sets in chic settings. This side of Brussels nightlife combines the festive season with the city's modern, cosmopolitan vibe.

Whether it's sipping a spiced Christmas beer in a century old pub, listening to a choir echo through a cathedral, or enjoying live music with friends, Brussels' nightlife in December captures the spirit of the holiday season. It strikes a balance between tradition and modernity, ensuring that each night spent in the city is as memorable as the day.

When night falls, Brussels transforms into a living canvas of light. The city's illuminations in December are more than just decorations; they are meticulously planned spectacles that transform historic landmarks, market squares, and streets into glowing works of art. For visitors who enjoy photographing memories, Brussels at night provides numerous opportunities to highlight the festive atmosphere in unique ways.

The Grand Place serves as the city's focal point after dark. Its UNESCO listed square, which is already stunning by day, becomes even more spectacular at night when a light and sound show illuminates the gilded guildhalls and the town hall. The massive Christmas tree and nativity scene in the center of the square provide depth and seasonal focus, resulting in postcard perfect shots. Photographers frequently linger here, capturing the contrast between warm golden lights and the deep winter sky.

Moving on to Place Sainte Catherine and Marché aux Poissons, the glow of the W\_\_\_\_. Wonders market is equally enchanting. Rows of wooden chalets, each illuminated with twinkling bulbs, create inviting scenes in which the details of handmade crafts and food stalls come to life in photographs. The Ferris wheel, with its ever changing colors, serves as both a subject and a vantage point; riding it provides sweeping nighttime views of the illuminated city below, ideal for panoramic shots.

Another highlight is the Boulevard Anspach, where the streets are decorated with festive garlands and overhead light installations. Walking through these decorated streets feels like entering a light tunnel, making it ideal for candid shots as well as dramatic compositions. Along with these, the Galeries Royales Saint Hubert, with its glass ceiling draped in garlands and golden tones, produces elegant interior shots, particularly for those who enjoy architectural photography.

For those seeking quieter moments, the Parc de Bruxelles and the areas surrounding the Royal Palace frequently feature subtle but beautifully arranged lighting, allowing for atmospheric photos away from the crowds. The reflection of lights on wet cobblestones after a light winter drizzle adds character, creating natural effects that improve night photography.

Capturing Brussels after dark does not necessitate professional equipment; smartphones frequently suffice, thanks to the city's powerful lighting displays. Photographers seeking sharper night shots, on the other hand, will benefit from using a tripod to steady long exposures, particularly when photographing the Grand Place's light shows or the Ferris wheel in motion. The interplay of shadow and illumination in historic architecture offers limitless creative opportunities for those willing to pause and frame their shots.

Brussels at night is a city that exudes character. Whether it's the grand spectacles in the squares, the cozy glow of markets, or the small details of festive shop windows, every corner has an image worth remembering. For visitors, walking with a camera after dark is more than just photography; it's about seeing the city from a perspective that combines history, tradition, and holiday magic in one frame.

# CHAPTER 6

## FAMILY FRIENDLY CHRISTMAS ACTIVITIES

**B**russels in December is especially welcoming to families, with activities that both children and adults can enjoy. The Winter Wonders festival is the epitome of family fun, with its sparkling Ferris wheel, ice skating rink, and colorful light parades that captivate children's imaginations. Families can wander through the Christmas market chalets, sampling waffles and hot chocolate and shopping for handmade gifts.

The Grand Place is another popular destination for children, who marvel at the towering Christmas tree and the animated light and sound show that brings the square to life. Nativity scenes, both traditional and creative, can be found throughout the city, offering cultural and festive storytelling opportunities for young visitors. A stroll through the decorated Parc de Bruxelles or a visit to local chocolate shops, where children can watch pralines being made, adds a sweet touch to the holiday experience.

With its blend of fun, wonder, and tradition, Brussels provides families with a warm and memorable Christmas experience that is both playful and enchanting.

Brussels is an excellent holiday destination for families, with numerous attractions to keep children entertained and engaged. Among the highlights are the city's festive ice rinks, charming carousels, and a variety of family-friendly activities that combine fun with the magic of Christmas.

The ice rink at Place de la Monnaie, in front of the Théâtre Royal de la Monnaie, serves as the focal point of family activities. Each December, the square is transformed into a bustling skating destination, complete with twinkling lights, festive music, and a happy crowd. Skaters of all ages take to the ice, with smaller sections or aids readily available for children who are just learning to skate. Parents can enjoy warm drinks from nearby stalls while keeping an eye on the action, making for a relaxing yet festive outing for the entire family.

Children are drawn to the traditional carousels set up around the market areas, particularly near Place Sainte Catherine, which are close to the Winter Wonders festivities. These rides are frequently designed with whimsical details, wooden animals, and glowing lights, making them a nostalgic favorite among both children and parents. The carousels are small but magical, providing a gentle thrill for younger children while contributing to the bustling market atmosphere.

Beyond the ice rink and carousels, Brussels has other family friendly attractions woven into the Winter Wonders experience. The Ferris wheel at Vismet is a popular family attraction, providing breathtaking views of the city lit up. On a clear night, children and adults can see the market chalets, the Grand Place, and even the Atomium. For children who enjoy spectacle, the light parades that pass through the market areas are filled with costumes, glowing figures, and festive music that create the atmosphere of a moving fairytale.

Smaller touches throughout the city keep children entertained. Nativity scenes, some with life-size figures or live animals, invite families to explore and tell stories together. Many stalls at the Winter Wonders market sell toys, sweets, and holiday trinkets suitable for younger visitors. In addition, several museums, such as the Belgian Comic Strip Center (Rue des Sables 20, 1000 Brussels), offer family friendly exhibits that provide a cozy break from outdoor activities while remaining true to the festive theme of imagination and wonder.

The ice rinks, carousels, and kid friendly attractions combine to make Brussels a city that brings Christmas to life for families. These activities are not only entertaining, but they also provide opportunities for children to share experiences that they will cherish. Whether it's skating under the lights, riding a carousel, or admiring the city from the Ferris wheel, Brussels ensures that its holiday celebrations are enjoyable for people of all ages.

### 6.2 Storytelling, puppet shows, and Santa encounters

Storytelling, Puppet Shows, and Santa Encounters
 Christmas in Brussels is more than just markets and lights; it's about traditions that bring stories to life for children and families. During the holiday season, the city provides a variety of cultural and entertaining experiences tailored specifically for young visitors, combining fun with seasonal magic. These events are frequently held within the Winter Wonders program or in cultural venues throughout the city, making them easy to incorporate into a family vacation itinerary.

## Storytelling Events

Brussels has a long tradition of oral storytelling, and December is when it really shines. Libraries, community centers, and cultural venues throughout the city host holiday storytelling afternoons where children can hear tales of Christmas legends, winter folklore, and Belgian traditions. These sessions are frequently interactive, encouraging children to participate, sing, or respond to the storyteller's prompts. The Maison du Livre (Rue de Rome 24, 1060 Brussels) is a popular venue that hosts seasonal reading events. Some market chalets even plan short readings of holiday stories to create cozy moments amidst the bustling atmosphere.

## Puppet shows

Brussels is known for its traditional puppet theatre, and the holiday season allows families to experience this beloved art form. The Royal Theatre Toone (Rue du Marché aux Herbes 66, 1000 Brussels) is the city's most famous puppet theatre, with a history that dates back to the nineteenth century. Its puppeteers perform adaptations of classic stories, often with a festive or humorous twist. Special shows are added to the program around Christmas, making it a favorite among both children and adults. The rustic atmosphere of the Toone Theatre, combined with the charm of handmade puppets, creates an experience that is both traditional and timeless.

*Santa Encounters*

No Christmas visit to Brussels is complete without meeting Santa Claus. During Winter Wonders, Santa makes regular appearances in his chalet, which is typically located near Place Sainte Catherine, where children can meet him, share their wishes, and take photos. His chalet is decorated like a winter cabin, adding to the allure of the encounter. Santa visits are also available at shopping centers such as City 2 (Rue Neuve 123, 1000 Brussels) and Galeries Royales Saint Hubert, which include festive photo corners and small gifts for children. These encounters are more than just photos; they are part of a larger festive story that will keep children entertained throughout their Brussels vacation.

Together, storytelling events, puppet shows, and Santa encounters make Brussels a city that not only celebrates Christmas, but also shares it with children through experiences that spark their imaginations. These traditions add layers of magic to the city's festive atmosphere, ensuring that young visitors leave with memories as enchanting as the lights and markets.

*6.3 Parks and fun winter spaces*

In between the bustling markets and glowing city squares, Brussels' parks and open spaces allow families and visitors to enjoy winter in a more relaxed, playful setting. These areas combine the charm of seasonal decorations with open air fun, giving children space to play and parents a break from the busier festive streets.

The Parc de Bruxelles (Warandepark, 1000 Brussels) is one of the most important spaces, located near the Royal Palace. During December, its tree lined paths are frequently adorned with subtle holiday lights, providing a serene backdrop for winter strolls. Families enjoy strolling through the park to admire the decorations or simply letting their children play in the open spaces while enjoying the fresh air. The park also provides a quieter retreat for visitors seeking a break from the bustling market crowds.

During the holidays, the nearby Mont des Arts transforms into a magical viewpoint. Though not a traditional park, its terraced gardens and open plaza are beautifully illuminated at night, providing children with play areas to explore as well as excellent photo opportunities for families. The steps and pathways offer both a scenic route and a sense of discovery, with the city skyline in the background glittering with holiday lights.

Parc du Cinquantenaire (1000 Brussels), with its grand arch and wide lawns, is another popular destination for those who enjoy combining culture and recreation. While less decorated than the central squares, it offers space for winter walks and family activities, particularly on sunny December days. The area surrounding the park occasionally hosts smaller festive events or pop up stalls, and children frequently enjoy simply running around in the open space after spending time in crowded markets.

During Winter Wonders, playful winter spaces expand beyond traditional parks. The ice rink at Place de la Monnaie and the bustling square at Vismet are both designed as festive playgrounds in their own right. Between skating, carousels, and seasonal rides, these areas serve as temporary "winter parks," where families can play, watch performances, and eat snacks under the glow of decorations.

The city's parks and playful spaces work together to create balance during a holiday in Brussels. They provide moments of calm and fun, allowing children to unwind while also providing families with an opportunity to explore Brussels beyond the markets. Whether it's sliding across the ice, running through tree lined paths, or admiring panoramic views, these winter destinations add warmth and joy to cold December days.

# CHAPTER 7

## ROMANTIC CHRISTMAS IN BRUSSELS

Brussels is a city that naturally lends itself to romance, and its allure grows stronger during the holiday season. Strolling hand in hand through the Grand Place, with its golden façades glowing under the light show and the towering Christmas tree in the center, is like entering a fairytale. Couples frequently find themselves wandering through the Galeries Royales Saint Hubert, where festive garlands and sparkling shop windows create a cozy, elegant atmosphere ideal for sharing hot chocolate or indulging in pralines.

Another highlight at Vismet is the Ferris wheel, which provides breathtaking views of the illuminated city skyline, making for an especially magical experience when shared with someone special. For a more tranquil escape, the paths of the Mont des Arts and Parc de Bruxelles offer peaceful walks framed by soft lights and winter air. Whether it's clinking glasses of mulled wine at a Christmas market chalet or dining by candlelight in a tucked away bistro, Brussels during the holidays creates a romantic atmosphere in simple but unforgettable ways.

A horse drawn carriage ride through Brussels' historic streets is one of the most enchanting ways to experience the city at Christmas. As the city twinkles with holiday lights, the gentle rhythm of hooves on cobblestones creates a timeless atmosphere, giving visitors a slower, more intimate view of the city's splendor. These rides are especially popular during the holiday season, when Brussels' squares and avenues are festooned with decorations and the crisp winter air adds to the ambiance.

The carriages usually leave from the Grand Place (1000 Brussels), the center of the city's celebrations. From here, the route winds through nearby medieval lanes, passing landmarks like the Bourse, Rue du Lombard, and the bustling streets surrounding Place Sainte Catherine. Along the way, passengers can see illuminated shop fronts, cozy cafés, and the Winter Wonders chalets. The ride emphasizes the contrast between Brussels' grand architectural gems and its narrow, winding alleys, providing a view that is difficult to capture on foot.

Carriages are typically decorated for the season, with warm blankets available to keep guests warm on chilly evenings. Drivers often dressed in traditional attire, share historical facts about the streets and buildings, adding a storytelling element to the journey. Couples find these rides particularly romantic, while families value the novelty and delight it provides for children.

The soundscape is also an integral part of the magic. As the carriage passes through the Christmas markets, the jingling of harness bells combines with carols and the hum of festive crowds. As the ride progresses through quieter streets, the pace slows, and the only sounds are the horse's hooves and the creak of the carriage wheels.

Practical details are simple: rides can be booked directly at the Grand Place departure point, with options ranging from short loops around the historic center to longer tours that visit more of the city's attractions. Prices vary depending on the length of the ride, but the experience is more about enjoying a festive tradition from another era.

A horse drawn carriage ride through Brussels during Christmas is more than just sightseeing; it's an immersion into the city's spirit. Wrapped in a blanket, watching the lights dance across centuries old buildings, visitors experience Brussels not only as it is today, but also as it could have been in the past: magical, atmospheric, and timeless.

## 7.2 Romantic dinner for two at cozy Belgian restaurants

Brussels is as much about flavors as it is about sights, and during the holidays, the city's restaurants transform into havens of warmth and intimacy. Dining at a cozy Belgian restaurant is one of the most romantic experiences the city has to offer. Candlelit tables, glowing interiors, and hearty winter dishes create an atmosphere in which time appears to slow, allowing you to savor both the food and the experience.

Many of the most charming options can be found in the Grand Place and Îlot Sacré quarters, where narrow cobblestone streets conceal small brasseries and family owned restaurants. Wooden beams, soft lighting, and holiday decorations make each space feel like you're walking into someone's home. Couples can eat Belgian classics like waterzooi (a creamy chicken or fish stew), carbonnade flamande (slow-cooked beef in dark beer), or roast game dishes, which are Christmas staples. Sharing a pot of steaming moules frites and a glass of Belgian beer adds a fun, traditional touch to the meal.

For a more refined experience, the Sablon district has elegant dining rooms that combine history and sophistication. Local dishes are frequently paired with fine wines or carefully selected Belgian beers at these restaurants. Many of them place a special emphasis on desserts, whether it's a plate of pralines from a nearby chocolatier or a warm, spiced tart to round out a festive day.

Winter also brings seasonal menus to many restaurants, including game meats, roasted turkey, and dishes infused with truffles or chestnuts. These are frequently accompanied by Christmas beers, which are rich, spiced brews meant to complement hearty winter flavors. Dining by a window overlooking decorated streets or next to a small crackling fireplace only heightens the intimacy.

Some restaurants, such as Le Roy d'Espagne (Grand Place 1, 1000 Brussels), combine atmosphere and iconic views, allowing couples to dine while looking out over the illuminated square. Others, such as small bistros hidden in the Marolles or near Place Sainte Catherine, offer quieter, less crowded environments that feel like well kept secrets.

Romantic dining in Brussels is more than just the food; it's also about the setting, the atmosphere, and the shared experience. Whether it's a rustic brasserie serving comfort food, an elegant restaurant serving fine seasonal menus, or a hidden bistro discovered on a winter stroll, the city welcomes couples to slow down, warm up, and connect over flavors that embody Belgian hospitality. In the glow of holiday lights and the warmth of a cozy dining room, a meal for two in Brussels becomes a memory to cherish long after the holidays are over.

## 7.3 Hidden corners and quiet escapes from the crowds

While December in Brussels is filled with festive markets, parades, and illuminated squares, there are also hidden gems where visitors can escape the crowds and enjoy the city's quieter charms. These escapes allow couples, families, and solo travelers to relax, soak up the atmosphere at their own pace, and experience a different side of Brussels' Christmas spirit.

The Beguinage Quarter, which includes the Church of Saint John the Baptist at the Béguinage (Place du Béguinage, 1000 Brussels), is one of the most peaceful places to wander. This area, surrounded by small streets and fewer crowds, exudes calm, especially when its square is softly lit in the winter evenings. It's a quiet place to admire architecture and get away from the hustle and bustle of the market.

The Galeries Royales Saint Hubert are frequently busy, but entering its side passages or smaller cafés tucked beneath its arches can feel like discovering a secret retreat. Couples frequently visit these locations for a quiet hot chocolate away from the bustle of the main halls. Similarly, the charming streets of the Marolles district offer a more relaxed atmosphere. Antique shops and hidden cafés invite leisurely browsing, providing a welcome respite from the festive frenzy in the city center.

For those seeking fresh air, the Mont des Arts gardens are especially peaceful in the early morning or late evening, when crowds are thinner. With panoramic views of the city and subtle holiday lighting, it's the ideal spot for quiet reflection or photography without distraction. Another option is the Jardin du Petit Sablon (Rue de la Régence, 1000 Brussels), a small landscaped park flanked by elegant statues and historic townhouses. During December, its tranquil atmosphere contrasts beautifully with the vibrant energy of nearby markets.

Even within the Winter Wonders celebrations, there are hidden corners. A short walk from the main clusters of chalets around Place Sainte Catherine, side streets frequently reveal smaller stalls, less crowded cafés, or quieter squares where holiday lights twinkle without the crowds. Visitors who venture a little further from the main paths frequently discover these more intimate experiences.

Parc Léopold (Rue Belliard, 1000 Brussels), near the European Quarter, offers a peaceful green space surrounded by historic buildings. In the winter, its frozen ponds and bare trees take on a serene beauty, providing a moment of peace away from the holiday rush.

These hidden gems remind visitors that Brussels' allure isn't just in its grand displays and bustling markets, but also in its ability to provide intimacy and peace. Whether sitting on a bench in a quiet park, exploring a hidden church, or sipping a warm drink in a side street café, these escapes provide balance to the holiday experience, making Brussels feel both vibrant and personal.

# CHAPTER 8

## SHOPPING AND CHRISTMAS GIFTS

Christmas shopping in Brussels is more about the experience than it is about finding the perfect gift. The city has a variety of festive markets, elegant boutiques, and specialty shops, making browsing enjoyable. Visitors to the Winter Wonders chalets can purchase handmade crafts, ornaments, candles, and artisanal food products that embody the season's spirit.

For luxury shopping, the Galeries Royales Saint Hubert (Galerie du Roi 5, 1000 Brussels) is a must see, with beautifully decorated arcades housing chocolatiers, jewelers, and fashion boutiques. Chocolates from world famous brands such as Neuhaus, Leonidas, and Pierre Marcolini are popular Belgian gifts, while smaller artisan shops offer unique pralines and truffles.

Antique enthusiasts and those looking for one of a kind finds can visit the Sablon district, which is known for its art galleries and weekend markets. Whether it's gourmet food baskets, festive beers, handmade lace, or fine art, Brussels provides thoughtful and memorable gifts that go above and beyond the typical holiday gift.

Brussels offers souvenirs that capture the essence of Belgian culture, craftsmanship, and culinary traditions. Visitors looking for meaningful gifts or keepsakes will discover that the city's specialties, such as chocolates, lace, and beers, are more than just products; they represent Belgian heritage and artistry.

### *Chocolates*

Belgium is known around the world for its fine chocolate, and Brussels is the country's indulgence capital. Visitors can choose from well known brands such as Neuhaus, which is credited with inventing the praline, and Pierre Marcolini, which is known for its refined, haute couture approach to chocolate making. Godiva and Leonidas remain popular for their affordable but high quality pralines and truffles. For those looking for something more artisanal, smaller chocolatiers like Laurent Gerbaud create unique blends with spices, fruits, and nuts. A box of Belgian pralines or a beautifully wrapped chocolate assortment is one of Brussels' most treasured gifts, representing luxury and tradition in a single bite.

### Lace

Belgian lace, while not as popular as chocolates, remains a specialty with centuries of tradition. Handmade lace, often intricate and delicate, reflects the artistry of places like Bruges and Brussels. Lace is sold in shops around the Grand Place in the capital, ranging from doilies and handkerchiefs to framed designs and wearable accessories. While machine made lace is more common and inexpensive, hand woven pieces are highly valued for their detail and craftsmanship. Maison Antoine, for example, sells authentic lace items that make timeless souvenirs, ideal for those who value fine craftsmanship and historical significance.

### Beers

Belgium's beer culture is recognized by UNESCO as part of the world's intangible heritage, making a selection of local brews a must have Brussels souvenir. Shops like Beer Mania and the famous Delirium Café sell an impressive selection of bottles to take home, including festive Christmas beers brewed exclusively for the winter season. These seasonal beers are typically dark, rich, and spiced with flavors such as cinnamon, clove, or caramel, making them ideal gifts for beer lovers. Many specialty shops also sell tasting sets or gift packs that allow customers to try a variety of styles, ranging from fruity lambics to strong Trappist ales.

Souvenirs in Brussels are more than just keepsakes; they represent the country's artistry, heritage, and love of quality. Whether it's a box of pralines tied with ribbon, a delicate lace ornament, or a pack of Christmas beers, these items capture the spirit of Belgium and make memorable gifts that keep the warmth of a Brussels Christmas alive long after the trip is over.

## 8.2 Where to Shop: Christmas Market vs. Luxury Boutiques

Brussels during the holiday season provides two very different but equally rewarding shopping experiences: the festive charm of the Christmas markets and the refined elegance of its luxury boutiques. Both appeal to different types of visitors, and together they paint a balanced picture of what Christmas shopping in Brussels can be like.

### Christmas market shopping

The Winter Wonders market, which runs from the Grand Place to the Place Sainte Catherine, is the hub of festive shopping in Brussels. Wooden chalets line the squares and streets, adorned with fairy lights and garlands, creating an atmosphere straight out of a holiday story. Visitors can browse a diverse selection of handcrafted items, seasonal decorations, and regional delicacies.

- Handmade Gifts: From knitted scarves and woolen mittens to wooden toys and ornaments, many stalls sell items created by local artisans. These distinctive, handcrafted items make thoughtful and personal keepsakes.
- Festive Food Products: Chalets selling jars of Belgian honey, spiced jams, speculoos cookies, and artisanal chocolates provide customers with locally flavored edible gifts.
- Seasonal Atmosphere: The joy of shopping here is not only in the purchase, but also in the overall experience of sipping mulled wine while browsing, listening to carolers, and watching children glide across the nearby skating rink.

The Christmas market is ideal for those looking to take home souvenirs that capture the warmth and spirit of Brussels' holiday season.

### Luxury boutiques

On the other end of the spectrum, Brussels is a top shopping destination for high end goods. The city's Galeries Royales Saint Hubert is a luxury shopping landmark, with a stunning 19th century glass roofed arcade filled with elegant boutiques, chocolate shops, and jewelers. For those looking for designer labels, Brussels offers a mix of international fashion houses and Belgian brands known for their craftsmanship.

- Fashion and Accessories: Avenue Louise is Brussels' equivalent to Paris' Champs Élysées. Luxury boutiques on this avenue include Louis Vuitton, Chanel, and Prada, as well as Belgian designers Ann Demeulemeester and Dries Van Noten.
- Jewelry and Lace: For exquisite gifts, boutiques in Galeries Saint Hubert and around the Grand Place sell Belgian lace and fine jewelry, which is frequently accompanied by impeccable service.
- Gourmet Chocolates: Luxury shopping also includes chocolate. Shops such as Pierre Marcolini and Wittamer create artisanal chocolates that are packaged like works of art and make ideal premium gifts.

Luxury shopping in Brussels offers a refined experience with beautifully decorated storefronts, attentive service, and products that value quality, tradition, and exclusivity.

Both the Christmas market and the boutiques highlight Brussels' identity in unique ways. The market embodies the communal, joyful spirit of the holidays with handcrafted goods and seasonal treats, while the boutiques provide elegance, refinement, and the timeless appeal of luxury. For many visitors, the magic of Christmas shopping in Brussels stems from the opportunity to purchase artisanal gifts at the market as well as a luxury item or two from the city's renowned boutiques.

### 8.3 Seasonal Sales and Holiday Shopping Tips

Brussels during the Christmas season is more than just festive lights and cozy markets; it's also a great time to shop. From handcrafted treasures at markets to high end fashion in boutiques, the city is brimming with opportunities to find unique gifts. Knowing how to navigate seasonal sales and where to find the best deals makes shopping easier and more rewarding.

### Timing your shopping

The Christmas season is divided into two major shopping periods. In December, stores and markets focus on holiday themed items like decorations, gourmet food, and winter fashion. Prices here are not always discounted, but they do reflect seasonal demand. Visitors who extend their stay until January, on the other hand, can take advantage of Belgium's official winter sales period, which usually begins in the first week of January and lasts the entire month. This is when high-end boutiques and department stores discount clothing, shoes, and accessories by up to 70%.

### Christmas Market Tips

- Arrive Early or Late: To avoid crowds, go to the Winter Wonders market in the late morning or later in the evening, when the lights are on but the busiest rush is over.
- Bring Cash: While many chalets now accept credit cards, smaller vendors still prefer cash.
- Sample Before Buying: Food items such as pralines, cheeses, and speculoos are frequently provided as samples. This allows you to select the freshest and most authentic gifts.
- Buy Local: Look for stalls operated by Belgian artisans. Handmade lace, pottery, and knitted accessories are more authentic and difficult to find outside the country.

### Shopping Tips for Boutiques and Malls

- Galeries Royales Saint Hubert: Ideal for high end gifts like artisanal chocolates, jewelry, and lace. Prices here reflect prestige, so compare boutiques before making major purchases.
- Avenue Louise is known for international luxury brands, as well as Belgian designers who may offer one of a kind pieces not found elsewhere.

- Sales in January: If luxury shopping is on your agenda, visiting during the winter sales will allow you to buy high end items at significantly lower prices.

### *General Holiday Shopping Advice*
- Dress Warmly: Although many shops remain open late in December, browsing the open air markets requires layers to stay comfortable.
- Prepare for crowds: Saturdays and Sundays are the busiest. Weekdays are quieter, which makes browsing easier.
- Consider Luggage Space: When purchasing chocolates or beer, keep in mind how much you can safely pack for transportation. Shops such as Neuhaus and Leonidas frequently offer travel friendly packaging.
- Keep an eye out for limited editions: Many Belgian chocolatiers and breweries release special Christmas editions that are typically only available during the holiday season. These make excellent collector's gifts.

Shopping in Brussels at Christmas combines festive charm with practical value. Visitors can get the best of both worlds by visiting the markets in December and timing their boutique purchases for winter sales in January.

# CHAPTER 9

## DAY TRIPS AND EXCURSIONS FROM BRUSSELS

Brussels is conveniently located for visiting nearby towns and attractions, making it ideal for day trips during the Christmas season. A short train ride or drive can transport visitors to charming Belgian cities, each with its own festive atmosphere.

Ghent is a medieval gem with cobblestone streets, canals, and a Christmas market on Sint Baafsplein, where lights sparkle on the waterways. Bruges, also known as the "Venice of the North," dazzles with its canals, historic squares, and a cozy Christmas market on Markt Square, creating a storybook winter scene.

For chocolate lovers, Antwerp has a mix of holiday markets and world class chocolatiers, whereas Leuven, known for its university and vibrant squares, has smaller, charming markets perfect for a quiet day trip.

These excursions allow visitors to explore Belgium beyond Brussels, combining historic architecture, festive traditions, and local delicacies, all within easy reach of the capital.

*9.1 Bruges: Fairytale Canals and Christmas Magic*
Bruges, located just over an hour by train from Brussels, is a must-see destination for anyone looking for a truly magical Christmas. Known as the "Venice of the North," this medieval city captivates visitors with its winding canals, cobblestone streets, and beautifully preserved historic buildings. During December, Bruges transforms into a winter wonderland, combining its timeless charm with the festive spirit of the season.

The Markt Square is the center of Bruges' Christmas festivities. A towering Christmas tree stands alongside rows of wooden chalets in the city's main market, which sells handmade crafts, seasonal treats, and holiday gifts. At night, the square is illuminated with soft golden lights that reflect off the surrounding Gothic façades, providing the ideal backdrop for holiday photos. A traditional ice rink is set up nearby, where families and couples can glide under strings of twinkling lights, adding an active and playful element to the city's holiday atmosphere.

Bruges' canals offer a unique view of the city at Christmas. Horse drawn carriage rides along cobblestone streets and canal bridges allow visitors to experience the city's charm at a slower, more intimate pace. Evening canal cruises provide reflections of illuminated medieval buildings on the water, creating the illusion of gliding through a moving postcard. These rides are especially magical in December, when the reflections of holiday lights and decorations create a dreamy atmosphere.

For those interested in culture, Bruges offers seasonal performances and concerts in its historic churches and theaters. The Basilica of the Holy Blood (Burg 13, 8000 Bruges), famous for its Holy Blood relic, frequently hosts holiday themed concerts, while local theaters and community halls host family friendly shows and nativity performances.

The culinary delights of Bruges complement its scenic beauty. Visitors can warm up with Belgian hot chocolate, eat freshly made waffles, or try speculoos and other seasonal pastries at market stalls. Many small restaurants and bistros in the city center serve hearty winter dishes such as game meats and seasonal stews, making them ideal for winding down after a day of exploring.

Bruges in December combines history, romance, and holiday cheer. Its canals, illuminated streets, and charming markets create a magical winter experience reminiscent of stepping into a storybook. A day trip to Bruges from Brussels allows visitors to experience the warmth, wonder, and timeless beauty of a Belgian Christmas far from the capital.

## 9.2 Ghent Castle Celebrations and Festive Lights

Ghent, just a short train ride from Brussels, is a vibrant city that seamlessly blends history, culture, and holiday spirit. During the Christmas season, the city transforms into a vibrant festive destination, combining medieval architecture with twinkling lights and seasonal festivities. Ghent, known for its impressive castle, canals, and bustling squares, provides visitors with a one of a kind holiday experience that combines tradition and modern celebrations.

The Gravensteen Castle serves as the focal point of Ghent's Christmas charm. During December, the castle frequently hosts seasonal events such as medieval themed markets, workshops, and performances that transport visitors back in time while celebrating the holiday season. Walking through its stone walls, which are adorned with festive garlands, visitors can imagine centuries old celebrations while enjoying modern seasonal treats from nearby stalls.

The city's Christmas market, located near Sint Baafsplein and Korenmarkt, features rows of wooden chalets selling handcrafted gifts, artisanal foods, and holiday decorations. The market is well known for its warm and welcoming atmosphere, which is enhanced by street performers, live music, and the aroma of mulled wine and roasted chestnuts in the air. Small rides and interactive stalls provide a playful element that keeps children entertained.

Ghent's canals and historic streets are adorned with extensive holiday lighting installations, which create stunning reflections in the water after dark. Walking along the canals, visitors can see illuminated bridges, decorative lampposts, and seasonal projections on buildings that highlight the city's Gothic and Renaissance architecture. Photography enthusiasts will find numerous opportunities to capture the magic of Ghent, especially in the evening, when lights shine off the water and the city's historic silhouettes are framed in gold and silver.

Cultural experiences enhance Ghent's Christmas offerings. Churches such as St. Nicholas' Church and St. Bavo Cathedral frequently host Christmas concerts, choral performances, and special nativity displays, offering a peaceful contrast to the bustling markets. Seasonal exhibitions or workshops are occasionally held in the city center's art galleries and museums, adding an educational and creative element to a festive visit.

Ghent is also well known for its festive cuisine. Market stalls sell Belgian waffles, speculoos cookies, and hot chocolate, while nearby restaurants serve traditional winter fare like hearty stews, roasted meats, and seasonal vegetables. Belgian Christmas beers are also popular in local pubs, adding a cozy touch to the city's festive atmosphere.

Visiting Ghent during the Christmas season offers an ideal blend of history, celebration, and visual splendor. From festive castle events to illuminated canals and bustling markets, the city provides a magical experience for couples, families, and solo travelers alike. A day trip from Brussels allows visitors to experience Ghent's distinct blend of medieval charm and modern holiday excitement, resulting in lasting memories of a Belgian Christmas.

Antwerp, known as the "diamond capital of the world," combines luxury shopping with festive holiday charm, making it an excellent choice for a Christmas Day trip from Brussels. In December, the city balances commercial sophistication with seasonal celebrations, providing visitors with both sparkling gems and cozy holiday experiences.

### Diamond Shopping

Antwerp's Diamond District, which surrounds Hoveniersstraat and Schupstraat, is well known for its high quality diamonds, jewelry, and watches. Visiting during the holiday season allows shoppers to combine sightseeing with luxury purchases, as many stores sell beautifully packaged gifts ideal for special occasions. Whether buying fine jewelry or simply window shopping, the district exudes opulence, which is enhanced by festive decorations and elegant storefront displays. Knowledgeable jewelers offer insights into the history and craftsmanship of diamonds, making even a casual visit both educational and visually impressive.

## Christmas Markets

Antwerp's Christmas market (Grote Markt and Handschoenmarkt) embodies the city's festive spirit through a mix of artisan chalets, seasonal treats, and fun attractions. Wooden stalls sell handmade gifts, decorations, and Belgian delicacies like waffles, pralines, and speculoos cookies. Ice skating, merry go rounds, and light displays are popular activities for families, while couples and solo travelers can stroll through the illuminated squares, sampling mulled wine and taking in the vibrant atmosphere.

The Meir shopping street, Antwerp's main commercial thoroughfare, is beautifully decorated for the holidays, with luxury boutiques and department stores paired with festive window displays. Visitors can shop for fashion, accessories, and chocolates while taking in the warm glow of the Christmas lights strung across the street. Small side streets and hidden courtyards lead to more intimate markets and quaint cafés, offering a quieter but equally festive shopping experience.

## Cultural highlights

In addition to shopping, Antwerp's historical landmarks enrich the holiday experience. The Cathedral of Our Lady (Onze Lieve

Vrouwekathedraal, Groenplaats 21, 2000 Antwerp) regularly hosts Christmas concerts and nativity displays. Nearby, the MAS Museum (Hanzestedenplaats 1, 2000 Antwerp) may host seasonal exhibitions that combine art, culture, and festive exploration into a single itinerary.

Antwerp's Christmas celebrations combine luxury and seasonal cheer. Visitors can admire diamond craftsmanship, shop along beautifully decorated streets, and immerse themselves in festive markets brimming with lights, aromas, and joyful energy. A day trip from Brussels offers travelers the opportunity to experience both the elegance and warmth of Antwerp's holiday celebrations, making it an ideal addition to Belgium's winter itinerary.

### 9.4 Leuven and Liège: regional festive highlights
While Brussels is the center of Belgium's Christmas celebrations, the nearby cities of Leuven and Liège provide charming, smaller scale holiday experiences that highlight regional traditions and create a more intimate festive atmosphere. Both cities are easily accessible by train from Brussels, making them ideal for day trips or short excursions over the holidays.

## Leuven: University Town Charm

Leuven, known for its prestigious university and youthful energy, provides a cozy Christmas atmosphere with a mix of historic architecture, vibrant squares, and holiday markets. The Leuven Christmas Market is centered on Muntstraat and Grote Markt, with wooden chalets selling handcrafted gifts, seasonal foods, and locally brewed beer.

- Festive Activities: Leuven hosts seasonal events like ice skating rinks, light installations in the squares, and family-friendly workshops where kids can make ornaments or holiday crafts.
- Historic Sights: The city's Town Hall (Grote Markt 10, 3000 Leuven), one of Belgium's most ornate Gothic buildings, has been beautifully illuminated for the season, providing a stunning backdrop for photos and a sense of holiday grandeur in a compact, walkable city centre.
- Culinary Treats: Leuven is known for its beer culture, and local Christmas markets serve seasonal brews alongside traditional Belgian snacks such as waffles, speculoos, and roasted chestnuts.

Leuven's appeal stems from its blend of historic elegance, student energy, and approachable markets, making it ideal for visitors seeking a lively but manageable festive atmosphere.

### *Liège: Walloon festivities*

Liège, in the Walloon region of Belgium, offers a unique Christmas experience, blending French speaking Belgian culture with festive traditions. Liège's Christmas Market (Place Saint Lambert) is Wallonia's largest, with over a hundred wooden chalets selling artisanal goods, gifts, and seasonal treats.

- Festive Atmosphere: The market is bustling with street performers, carolers, and illuminated displays. A traditional ice skating rink and carousel entertain families, and seasonal light projections across the square add to the magical atmosphere.

- Regional Specialties: Liège is well-known for its gaufres de Liège (Liege waffles), which are heavier and caramelized than Brussels style waffles and can be found at market stalls throughout. Other Walloon delicacies, such as boulets à la Liégeoise (meatballs in a rich sauce) and speculoos, can be enjoyed on a walk.

- Cultural Highlights: Visitors can discover Liège's historic sites, including the Liège Cathedral, which frequently hosts Christmas concerts and seasonal events. The Montagne de Bueren, a famous steep staircase, provides panoramic views of the city decked out in holiday lights, making for a memorable photo opportunity.

Both Leuven and Liège offer regional Christmas experiences to complement the grandeur of Brussels. Leuven exudes a historic, youthful charm with approachable markets and vibrant energy, whereas Liège celebrates Wallonia's festive traditions with lively markets, culinary delights, and illuminated skylines. Visiting these cities allows visitors to experience Belgium's diverse holiday culture, ranging from Flemish charm to Walloon warmth, all within easy reach of the capital.

# CHAPTER 10

## PRACTICAL TRAVEL TIPS

Visiting Brussels during Christmas is magical, but a few practical tips can make your trip go more smoothly and enjoyably. December weather is cold and damp, so layering is essential, along with a warm coat, scarf, gloves, and waterproof shoes for walking on cobblestones.

Transportation throughout the city is convenient. Trams, buses, and metro lines connect major squares, markets, and tourist attractions, and many central areas are pedestrian friendly. Trains from Brussels Central Station provide convenient access to cities such as Bruges, Ghent, Antwerp, Leuven, and Liège. Crowd management is critical; weekends are the busiest times at markets and popular attractions, so visiting early in the day or late in the evening can be more enjoyable. Many attractions and stalls accept credit cards, but having some cash on hand is beneficial for small purchases.

*Finally*, make plans for dining and special events. Restaurants fill up quickly during the holiday season, and popular events like ice skating and carriage rides may require reservations. Being prepared allows you to fully experience Brussels' festive magic without stress.

Brussels is a festive wonderland during the holiday season, but the timing of your visit can make a big difference. Understanding the best times to visit, as well as peak times for attractions, allows visitors to enjoy the city while making the most of its seasonal offerings.

### Ideal dates

The festive season in Brussels typically lasts from late November to early January, with the exact dates of Winter Wonders and associated Christmas markets changing slightly each year. The Winter Wonders festival is scheduled to begin in the last week of November and run until the first week of January in 2025-2026.

- Early December (Weekdays): This time is ideal for visitors looking for a more relaxed experience. Markets are fully operational, decorations are in place, and the city is bustling without being overcrowded.
- Mid December: The festive spirit peaks as locals and tourists flock to the markets, ice rinks, and light displays. Visiting during the week allows

90

for enjoyable exploration, but weekends are noticeably busier.

- Late December (Christmas and New Year's): These days provide the most complete experience of holiday traditions, with special concerts, parades, and seasonal events. Expect crowded markets, higher lodging costs, and long wait times at popular attractions. While it is the most magical time, careful preparation is required to avoid frustration.
- Early January (Post Holiday Season): For those who prefer quieter streets, post Christmas visits are ideal. The decorations are still up, but the crowds have diminished significantly. In addition, this is the start of Belgium's winter sales, which provide discounted shopping opportunities in boutiques and department stores.

### Peak times during the day

- Evenings (5 p.m. - 9 p.m.): The best time to see light shows, illuminated facades, and Christmas decorations. However, evenings are also peak times for major squares such as the Grand Place.
- Late Morning to Early Afternoon (10 AM - 2 PM): Perfect for exploring markets, museums, and family-friendly activities with fewer people.

Cafés and restaurants are less crowded than in the evening rush.

- Weekends vs. Weekdays: Weekends attract both local families and international visitors, resulting in vibrant but crowded conditions. Weekdays are preferable for those looking for a more relaxed and flexible experience.

### *Special Considerations*

- Weather: December in Brussels is cold, with average temperatures ranging from 2°C to 6°C (36°F to 43°F) and occasional rain or light snow. It is recommended that you dress in layers, wear waterproof footwear, and carry an umbrella.
- Events: Some events, such as the Grand Place light show, ice skating tournaments, or concerts, may require reservations or tickets, particularly on busy days. Planning ahead of time ensures that you will have access without disappointment.
- Public Holidays: Belgium celebrates holidays such as Christmas Day and New Year's Day, during which some shops and services may close, while tourist attractions and markets remain partially open but crowded.

By scheduling your visit around these ideal dates and understanding peak times, you can make the most of Brussels' festive magic. Weekdays in early December and early January provide the best balance of a full holiday experience with manageable crowds, whereas evenings and weekends provide the spectacular sights that make the city so enchanting during Christmas.

## 10.2 Navigating the city during Christmas crowds

Brussels in December is a city ablaze with lights, music, and festive spirit. While this creates a magical atmosphere, it also means that popular areas, particularly the Grand Place, Place Sainte Catherine, and nearby Winter Wonders markets, can become extremely congested. Knowing how to navigate the city efficiently allows visitors to enjoy the festivities without feeling stressed.

### Public Transportation Tips

Brussels has a well connected public transportation system operated by STIB/MIVB, which includes trams, buses, and metro lines. During the holiday season, public transportation remains one of the quickest ways to get to key attractions while avoiding the traffic on crowded streets.

- Metro: Lines 1 and 5 connect central hubs, including the Gare de Bruxelles Central, providing easy access to the Grand Place and nearby markets.

- Trams and buses: Trams 3, 4, and 7, as well as buses 38 and 95, provide service to major shopping areas, Christmas markets, and cultural attractions. Evening schedules are slightly extended during Winter Wonders, but it is recommended that you check the timetable ahead of time.
- Tickets: Single tickets, day passes, or multi-day passes can be purchased at stations or through the STIB app, saving time over buying individual tickets during peak hours.

### Walking Tips for Crowded Areas:
- Begin Early: Visiting markets and squares in the morning allows for a more leisurely experience before the crowds arrive in the late afternoon and evening.
- Stick to Side Streets: While main squares like the Grand Place are must see, nearby streets like Rue des Bouchers or the alleys surrounding Galeries Royales Saint Hubert provide more intimate shopping, dining, and festive experiences.
- Plan Your Route: Identify key points of interest and create a walking route to reduce backtracking and avoid congested areas.

### Using Ride Sharing and Taxis

- Ride Sharing Apps: Services like Uber are available in Brussels and can be useful for short trips, particularly when transporting purchases or traveling with family.
- Taxis: Official taxis are available at designated stands, but traffic congestion may cause travel delays during peak market hours. It is recommended that you book your evening trips in advance.

### Timing Considerations:

- Evening Light Shows: Events such as the Grand Place light show draw large crowds. Arrive 30-45 minutes early to secure a good viewing spot, and evenings later in the week may be slightly less crowded than weekends.
- Lunch and Dinner Hours: Restaurants near the markets get busy quickly. Making reservations or dining slightly earlier (around 11:30 AM-12 PM or 5 PM-6 PM) helps to avoid long wait times.
- Weekday Visits: When possible, plan visits to popular attractions and markets on weekdays, as they are much less crowded than weekends.

Safety and Comfort

- Keep an eye on your belongings: Pickpockets prefer crowded areas. Keep valuables close by using crossbody bags or zipped backpacks.
- Dress in Layers: Crowds can slow movement and extend walking times, so warm clothing and waterproof shoes are essential for comfort.
- Take Breaks: Cafés, museums, and side streets offer opportunities to rest while enjoying festive sights, reducing fatigue in congested areas.

Visitors to Brussels can easily navigate the city during the busy Christmas season by combining public transportation, strategic walking routes, and timing. With proper planning and awareness, you can enjoy the city's festive lights, markets, and cultural highlights without feeling overwhelmed, resulting in a memorable and stress free holiday experience.

*10.3 Currency, cards, and budgeting fundamentals*
Visiting Brussels during the Christmas season necessitates some practical financial planning, such as understanding the local currency, payment methods, and typical costs. This ensures that shopping, dining, and seasonal activities run smoothly.

Belgium has the Euro (€) as its official currency. Banknotes have denominations of 5, 10, 20, 50, 100, 200, and 500 euros, while coins range from 1 cent to 2 euros. Prices in markets, shops, restaurants, and attractions are displayed in euros, and international visitors can complete the majority of transactions easily.

*Exchange Tips:* While exchanging money at airports or hotels is convenient, the fees are usually higher. ATMs in the city center or banks offer better rates.

*Small Change:* It is recommended that you bring some coins or small notes, especially for market stalls, street food, and tips.

### Card and Digital Payments

- Brussels is modern and card-friendly, but knowing what to expect can help avoid inconveniences.
- Credit and debit cards: Major credit cards, such as Visa, MasterCard, and Maestro, are widely accepted in restaurants, stores, and museums. Some smaller stalls at Christmas markets may prefer cash.
- Contactless Payments: Most businesses and cafes accept contactless payments, including mobile wallets like Apple Pay and Google Pay.

This is ideal for small purchases such as coffee, snacks, and souvenirs.

- ATMs are easily accessible throughout the city, including near the Grand Place, Gare de Bruxelles Central, and major shopping districts. Withdrawals typically yield a higher exchange rate than currency exchange counters.

### *Budgeting Basics*

The cost of a holiday in Brussels varies according to your travel style. Here's the general breakdown:

- Accommodation: Budget hotels or guesthouses: €70-€120 per night; mid range hotels: €120-€200; luxury hotels near Grand Place: €250 or more.
- Dining: Casual cafés or market stalls: €8-€20 per meal; mid range restaurants: €25-50 per person; fine dining: €60 or more. Seasonal menus or festive dinners may cost more, particularly in December.
- Attractions & Activities: Grand Place light shows are free; Winter Wonders ice skating: €5-€10 per person; Ferris wheel or other rides: €8-€12; museums: €10-€15 on average.
- Transportation: Single public transport tickets cost €2.50; day passes cost €7-€8; taxis or ride sharing prices vary but typically range between

€3 and €5, with additional charges per kilometer.

### *Tips for Budgeting:*
- Allow for additional spending on souvenirs, chocolates, and festive treats.
- Add in small expenses for hot drinks, snacks, or market purchases.
- Keep cash on hand for small vendors and to tip at restaurants or carriage rides.

Understanding currency, card usage, and typical holiday expenses enables visitors to enjoy Brussels' festive offerings with confidence. With a little planning, you can enjoy the experiences, markets, lights, and seasonal delights without worrying about practical financial matters.

# CHAPTER 11

## WHERE TO STAY DURING THE HOLIDAYS

Finding the right place to stay in Brussels during the Christmas season can significantly improve your holiday experience. The city has a variety of accommodations, ranging from charming boutique hotels to modern, centrally located options, all of which serve as a convenient base for exploring holiday markets, light displays, and cultural attractions.

For those who want to be in the thick of it, staying near the Grand Place or Place Sainte Catherine puts you within walking distance of the Winter Wonders, illuminated squares, and popular restaurants and cafés. This area is ideal for visitors who enjoy walking through festive streets several times per day and want easy access to the city's main attractions.

If you want a quieter stay while still being close to the festive atmosphere, Sablon and the Marolles district have boutique hotels and guesthouses tucked away on charming cobblestone streets. These areas offer a more intimate, peaceful atmosphere while keeping markets, museums, and restaurants within easy reach.

For families or those looking for modern amenities, the European Quarter and the areas surrounding Brussels Central Station offer easy access to public transportation, allowing for day trips to nearby cities such as Bruges, Ghent, and Antwerp. Many hotels in these areas provide larger rooms, family friendly services, and occasionally festive packages or special holiday decorations.

Brussels offers accommodations to suit every taste and budget, from luxury hotels with historic charm and panoramic city views to smaller guesthouses that feel cozy and personal. Choosing the right area and type of lodging allows visitors to fully experience the magic of the city's Christmas celebrations, whether they are looking for vibrant energy, quiet retreats, or easy access to both.

## 11.1 Best neighborhoods for a festive atmosphere

Brussels transforms into a holiday wonderland in December, and while the entire city exudes festive cheer, some neighborhoods stand out for their vibrant Christmas spirit, enchanting lights, and bustling markets. Exploring these areas allows visitors to fully immerse themselves in the seasonal atmosphere, whether they are shopping for gifts, eating delicious food, or simply strolling through illuminated streets.

## *Grand Place and Surroundings*

The Grand Place is the center of Brussels' Christmas festivities. This area, surrounded by ornate guildhalls and the striking Town Hall, serves as the Winter Wonders center. The main Christmas tree, seasonal lights, and nightly light shows form a magical focal point that attracts people from all over. Side streets like Rue des Bouchers and Rue du Marché aux Herbes are lined with boutiques, cafés, and chocolate shops that sell holiday treats and gifts. The combination of historic architecture and sparkling decorations makes this neighborhood a must see for anyone looking for a traditional Brussels holiday experience.

Place St. Catherine and the Port Area

Just a short walk from the Grand Place, the Place Sainte Catherine hosts a Winter Wonders market with artisan chalets, seasonal foods, and family friendly attractions. The nearby Sablon district, with its antique shops and cozy cafés, has a quieter, more sophisticated atmosphere while still adorned with holiday lights. This area is ideal for visitors who want to experience the festive energy of markets without the intensity of the main square.

### Sablon District
Sablon, known for its chocolate shops, art galleries, and historic architecture, exudes a refined and cozy holiday atmosphere. During December, the streets are illuminated with twinkling lights, and many stores have festive window displays. The neighborhood's blend of charm, elegance, and local culture makes it ideal for leisurely strolls, intimate dining, and discovering unique gifts.

### Marolles District
The Marolles neighborhood offers a more authentic and local experience. Known for its antique markets and quirky shops, this neighborhood comes to life during the holidays with street decorations, pop up stalls, and a welcoming atmosphere. Its slightly off the beaten path charm makes it an excellent place to explore away from the busiest tourist areas, while remaining within walking distance of the main festivities.

### European Quarter, Mont des Arts
For visitors who enjoy scenic views and a more relaxed festive atmosphere, the European Quarter and the Mont des Arts gardens provide wide streets,

elegant buildings, and seasonal light displays that are less crowded than the city center. Mont des Arts offers panoramic views of the city and is beautifully illuminated at night, making it an ideal location for evening walks or photography.

These neighborhoods work together to provide a complete holiday experience in Brussels. From the bustling energy of the Grand Place to the quiet charm of Marolles or the elegance of Sablon, each area adds to the city's festive atmosphere, providing visitors with a variety of markets, lights, dining, and cultural experiences that capture the magic of a Belgian Christmas.

## 11.2 Top Hotels With Christmas Charm

Brussels has a variety of hotels that go beyond just providing comfortable accommodations; they celebrate the holiday season with festive décor, special seasonal packages, and proximity to the city's Christmas attractions. Staying at one of these hotels allows visitors to fully immerse themselves in Brussels' magical atmosphere in December.

### Hotel Amigo

The Hotel Amigo, located just steps from the Grand Place, combines historic elegance with modern luxury. During the Christmas season, the lobby and public areas are decorated with seasonal items, creating a welcoming atmosphere. Guests can enjoy holiday packages that include chocolates, mulled wine, and recommendations for visiting the nearby Winter Wonders market. Its central location allows visitors to enjoy the Grand Place light shows and surrounding Christmas markets without having to walk long distances or take public transportation.

### The Hotel Bruxelles
The Hotel Brussels, located near Mont des Arts (Boulevard de Waterloo 38, 1000 Brussels), offers contemporary rooms with panoramic views of the city's holiday lights. During the holiday season, the hotel decor includes elegant touches like Christmas trees, wreaths, and themed amenities. Guests can unwind in the rooftop bar while admiring sweeping views of illuminated streets and nearby landmarks, making it an excellent choice for couples looking for a romantic getaway.

### Warwick Brussels – Grand Place
Warwick Brussels (Rue de la Montagne 17, 1000 Brussels) is another excellent choice for travelers seeking both convenience and a festive atmosphere. Its central location provides easy access to the Grand Place and nearby markets. During the

holiday season, the hotel decorates the public areas with Christmas trees and seasonal accents. Comfortable rooms, attentive service, and proximity to holiday events make it a popular choice for both families and couples.

### Steigenberger Wilcher's

Steigenberger Wiltcher's, located at Avenue Louise 71, 1050 Brussels, offers luxurious accommodations in one of the city's most elegant neighborhoods. During the holidays, the hotel's grand lobby and reception areas are transformed with festive décor, including beautifully decorated trees and seasonal lighting. Its location is ideal for exploring luxury boutiques on Avenue Louise and doing quieter, more stylish holiday shopping away from the busiest tourist areas.

### NH Collection Brussels Grand Sablon

Located in the heart of the Sablon district (Rue de la Régence 3, 1000 Brussels), this hotel provides a cozy, intimate atmosphere with festive touches in December. Guests can explore nearby chocolate shops, antique boutiques, and small holiday markets before returning to a lobby decorated with seasonal ornaments and lights. The combination of boutique charm and modern comfort makes it ideal for those looking for a more relaxed, culturally rich Christmas experience.

These hotels offer more than just a place to sleep; they also enhance the holiday experience with seasonal decorations, festive amenities, and prime locations that place guests in the heart of Brussels' Christmas magic. Choosing a Christmas themed hotel ensures that the city's lights, markets, and festive spirit are always nearby.

### 11.3 Cozy boutique stays versus luxury hotels

Brussels has a wide range of accommodations to suit all travelers, especially during the holiday season. Choosing between a cozy boutique stay and a luxury hotel comes down to the type of experience you seek, the atmosphere you prefer, and the balance of intimacy and extravagance. Both options have distinct advantages during the holiday season, each of which enhances your visit differently.

### Cozy Boutique Stays

Boutique hotels and guesthouses in Brussels frequently offer a more personalized and intimate experience. Many are housed in historic buildings with charming architecture, exposed beams, or distinctive design elements that reflect the city's personality. During the holidays, these accommodations frequently feature warm seasonal décor, such as small Christmas trees, wreaths, or subtle festive touches in common areas and rooms.

- Neighborhood Charm: Boutique stays are frequently located in quieter neighborhoods such as Sablon, Marolles, or near Mont des Arts, offering a peaceful respite after exploring bustling markets and squares. Guests can enjoy walking through cobblestone streets, discovering hidden chocolate shops, and visiting local cafés away from the crowds.
- Personalized Service: Smaller businesses allow employees to provide personalized attention, such as recommending local holiday events or arranging special seasonal amenities. Some boutique hotels even provide intimate winter packages, such as chocolate tastings, mulled wine, and guided walks through festive areas.
- Cultural Immersion: Staying in a boutique hotel allows guests to immerse themselves more directly in Brussels' culture, with local design, artwork, and architecture that highlight the city's history. This creates a homey, cozy atmosphere ideal for travelers who prefer charm and authenticity to grandeur.

### *Luxury Hotels*

Luxury hotels in Brussels combine elegance, grandeur, and a wide range of modern amenities. These accommodations are typically centrally located, such as near the Grand Place or Avenue Louise, allowing guests to easily access Christmas markets, light shows, and cultural attractions.

- Festive Elegance: In December, luxury hotels frequently decorate extensively for the holidays, with large Christmas trees, lavish wreaths, and professionally arranged seasonal displays in lobbies and public areas. This creates a fully immersive festive experience from the moment guests enter.

- Premium Services: High end hotels offer concierge services, fine dining restaurants, spas, and rooftop bars with spectacular views of the city lights. Many provide holiday packages that include special seasonal menus, gift baskets, and exclusive access to events.

- Convenience and Comfort: With large rooms, attentive staff, and modern amenities, luxury hotels are ideal for travelers looking for a stress free experience. They are also well suited for families, couples, and solo travelers seeking indulgence and comfort during the hectic Christmas season.

## Making the Choice

For Charm and Authenticity: Boutique stays provide a cozy, intimate, and culturally rich experience, making them ideal for travelers who enjoy exploring quieter streets, local shops, and hidden gems in the city.

For Grandeur and Convenience: Luxury hotels offer a lavish, all inclusive experience that includes easy access to central attractions, extensive amenities, and expertly curated holiday décor.

During the Christmas season in Brussels, both cozy boutique accommodations and luxury hotels offer memorable experiences. The decision is based on whether you value personal charm, cultural immersion, and a quiet ambiance over opulence, convenience, and festive spectacle. Many visitors discover that staying in a boutique hotel while exploring central markets and luxury shopping districts provides the best of both worlds.

### 11.4 Family friendly and affordable lodging options

Brussels has a diverse range of accommodations to suit families and budget conscious travelers, allowing you to experience the city's Christmas magic without breaking the bank. These options put comfort, convenience, and accessibility first, while still providing a festive atmosphere and easy access to the city's markets, light displays, and cultural attractions.

### Family Friendly Stays

Space, amenities, and convenience are key features of family friendly accommodations. Many mid range hotels and serviced apartments provide larger rooms or suites, which often include separate sleeping areas for children. Some properties offer family friendly amenities such as cribs, high chairs, and kids' entertainment programs.

- Location Matters: Families will appreciate neighborhoods such as Sablon, Mont des Arts, and those near Gare de Bruxelles Central. These areas provide easy walking access to markets, Christmas lights, and public transportation for day trips, while maintaining a more tranquil atmosphere away from the busiest crowds.
- On Site Amenities: During the holiday season, family friendly hotels frequently provide play areas, children's common rooms, or small indoor activities. Breakfasts may include kid friendly options, and some hotels even provide special holiday treats such as cookies or hot chocolate to younger guests.
- Market Proximity: Staying near Winter Wonders, Place Sainte Catherine, or the Grand

Place allows families to enjoy the ice rink, Ferris wheel, and carousels without having to travel long distances, making festive outings more convenient and enjoyable.

### *Budget Accommodation Options:*

Budget accommodations offer essential comforts at reasonable prices for travelers looking to experience Brussels' festive charm without breaking the bank. Hostels, budget hotels, guesthouses, and short term rentals are all possible options.

- Hostels and Guesthouses: Modern hostels in central locations, such as near Brussels Central Station, offer shared or private rooms, communal kitchens, and social areas, which are frequently decorated with holiday touches in December. Guesthouses in neighborhoods such as Marolles provide comfortable rooms with personal touches at reasonable rates.
- Short Term Rentals: Platforms such as Airbnb or local apartment rentals provide affordable options for groups or families, with kitchen facilities and flexible check in times. Staying in residential areas allows visitors to have a more authentic local experience while keeping costs low.
- Saving Tip: Book early during the holiday season because rooms fill up quickly. Choosing

accommodations slightly outside of the busiest tourist areas can also save money while maintaining easy access via public transportation.

- Brussels' family friendly and budget accommodations strike a balance of comfort, accessibility, and affordability. Families benefit from larger rooms, convenient locations, and festive touches that make holiday activities more enjoyable, while budget travelers can find cozy, well located options that let them experience the magic of Brussels' Christmas markets, lights, and seasonal charm without breaking the bank.

## 11.5 Emergency Contacts, Embassies, and Helplines

Visiting Brussels during the Christmas season is generally safe and enjoyable, but travelers should be prepared with key emergency contacts, embassy information, and helpline numbers. Having this information on hand allows for a quick response in the event of a medical emergency, lost documents, or other unforeseen circumstances.

### Emergency Services

- Police (Urgent Assistance): Call 101 for local police emergencies. Police stations can be found throughout the city, including in central areas near Grand Place and the Gare de Bruxelles Central.

- Fire Brigade: Call 100 in the event of a fire, an accident, or a hazardous situation.
- Medical Emergencies / Ambulance: Call 112, the general European emergency number, for ambulance and immediate medical assistance. This number works on both landlines and mobile phones.

### Hospitals and Medical Care

Brussels has several major hospitals equipped for emergencies.

- Cliniques Universitaires Saint Luc (Avenue Hippocrate 10, 1200 Woluwe Saint Lambert) provides comprehensive emergency services and employs English speaking staff.
- CHU Brugmann (Place Arthur Van Gehuchten 4, 1020 Brussels) - A central hospital providing emergency care.
- Hôpital Erasme (Route de Lennik 808, 1070 Brussels) is equipped to handle urgent medical situations and large scale emergencies.

Pharmacies are also readily available, with many open during the day and a few providing 24 hour service. Seasonal hours may vary, so check local listings or contact the hotel concierge.

### Embassies and Consulates

Knowing the location of your country's embassy or consulate can be critical for international travelers if passports are lost, legal issues arise, or immediate assistance is required.

United States Embassy: Boulevard du Régent 27, 1000 Brussels; phone: +32 2 811 4000.

United Kingdom Embassy: Avenue des Arts 50, 1000 Bruxelles - Phone: +32 2 287 6100.

Canadian Embassy: Avenue des Arts 50, 1000 Brussels; phone: +32 2 508 2500.

Most embassies are open during regular business hours, but many offer 24 hour emergency numbers for citizens abroad. It is best to register with your embassy before traveling to ensure prompt assistance.

### Tourist and travel helplines

Visit Brussels Tourist Information: +32 2 279 43 00 for information on attractions, directions, and festival updates.

STIB/MIVB Public Transport Information: +32 70 23 2000 - Helps you navigate trams, buses, and metro lines during the busy holiday season.

### Practical Tips

Keep a printed copy of your emergency numbers, embassy contact information, and hotel address.
Keep important phone numbers on your mobile device and record local emergency dialing codes.
If traveling with family, locate the nearest hospital or pharmacy to your lodging in advance.

Being prepared with emergency contacts, embassy information, and helplines ensures peace of mind while visiting Brussels during the holiday season. With these resources at their disposal, visitors can enjoy Christmas markets, light displays, and cultural experiences while knowing that assistance is available if necessary.

# CHAPTER 12

## WEATHER AND PACKING GUIDE

Decemberin Brussels is cold and frequently damp, with average temperatures ranging from 2°C to 6°C (36°F to 43°F). Rain is common, with the occasional light snowfall, creating a festive but chilly atmosphere. Daylight hours are limited, so planning indoor and evening activities is critical.

When packing, layering is essential. Warm sweaters, a waterproof coat, scarves, gloves, and a hat are essential for staying comfortable while exploring markets and walking around town. Waterproof shoes or boots with good traction are recommended for cobblestone streets. Additional layers and warm accessories ensure comfort during evening outings, particularly when viewing light displays.

A small backpack or cross body bag is ideal for carrying essentials such as an umbrella, snacks, and souvenirs. Packing for warmth and mobility allows visitors to fully enjoy Brussels' festive charm while remaining comfortable in the winter weather.

*12.1 What to expect from Brussels' winter climate*
Brussels has a typical temperate maritime climate, which becomes noticeably chilly in December, the height of the winter season. Understanding what to expect weather wise allows visitors to plan their clothing, daily activities, and travel schedules to make the most of the city's Christmas celebrations.

In December, temperatures in Brussels range from 4°C to 6°C (39°F-43°F) during the day and 0°C to 2°C (32°F-36°F) at night. Although it rarely drops to extreme lows, the dampness can make it feel colder than the thermometer shows. Layering with thermal undergarments and insulating outerwear is essential for comfort during long outdoor excursions, such as visiting Winter Wonders or exploring illuminated streets.

### *Precipitation and humidity*
December is one of Brussels' wettest months, with frequent light rain, drizzle, and snow flurries. Humidity levels are generally high, which can make the cold feel harsher. Waterproof coats, umbrellas, and water-resistant footwear are recommended for staying dry while visiting open air markets and street events. Snow is possible, but it is usually light and sporadic, which often adds to the city's festive atmosphere.

### Daylight hours

Brussels has short days in December, with daylight lasting approximately 8 to 9 hours. Sunrise is around 8:30 a.m., and sunset is around 4:30 p.m., so much of the city's winter charm is best enjoyed in the late afternoon and evening, when Christmas lights, illuminated façades, and light shows are visible. Indoor activities, such as museum visits or festive dining, are best planned during the day to ensure comfort while minimizing exposure to the colder parts of the day.

### Wind and Chill Factor

While Brussels is not particularly windy, exposed areas near open squares, canals, or elevated streets, such as Mont des Arts, may feel colder due to gentle winter breezes. A scarf, gloves, and a hat are essential for staying warm, especially on evening walks to view light displays or evening markets.

### Seasonal considerations

- Comfortable footwear: The streets are frequently wet, and the cobblestones can be slippery. Waterproof shoes with good traction reduce discomfort and accidents.

- Layering: Having multiple layers allows for easy transitions between indoor and outdoor temperatures. Lightweight sweaters, thermal tops, and a warm coat offer versatility.
- Evening Outfits: Extra layers, gloves, and scarves are recommended for shopping, ice skating, and watching light shows after dark.

Visitors to Brussels in December should be prepared for cool, damp weather, short daylight hours, and occasional snow, as well as to enjoy the festive atmosphere created by the city's winter climate. With appropriate clothing and planning, the cold can be part of the holiday charm, allowing visitors to fully enjoy Brussels' lights, markets, and seasonal events.

## 12.2 Essential packing checklist (layers, rainproof gear, and cozy accessories)

To stay warm, dry, and comfortable while exploring Brussels' festive attractions during the Christmas season, plan ahead of time. Layering is essential because it allows you to adjust to the changing temperatures between indoor warmth and chilly outdoor streets. To retain heat, start with thermal undergarments or lightweight base layers, then add sweaters, cardigans, or fleece for insulation. A good winter coat that is both warm and water resistant is essential for protecting against rain, snow, and damp winter air, which can make temperatures feel colder than they actually are.

Rainproof clothing is essential because the December weather in Brussels is frequently wet. A compact, sturdy umbrella and waterproof shoes or boots with good traction will allow you to navigate cobblestone streets and market areas comfortably. Gloves, scarves, and hats not only keep you warm but also provide comfort on long walks through illuminated squares, festive markets, or while waiting for light shows. Cozy accessories, such as wool socks or earmuffs, can make a significant difference in protecting extremities from the cold.

A small backpack or cross-body bag is ideal for carrying essentials like an umbrella, water bottle, snacks, or souvenirs from markets. Don't forget to pack chargers, travel documents, and a reusable shopping bag for unexpected purchases. Thoughtful packing allows visitors to fully experience Brussels' holiday magic, moving seamlessly between markets, light displays, and cultural attractions while remaining warm, dry, and comfortable throughout their festive adventures.

Visiting Brussels during the Christmas season is as much about enjoying the festive sights as it is about taking memorable photographs. The city's winter chill and damp conditions necessitate careful clothing selection, not only for warmth and comfort, but also for fashion and photography. Thoughtful holiday fashion allows you to move freely, stay comfortable, and appear festive in photos.

Layering is the cornerstone of winter fashion in Brussels. Begin with a lightweight thermal base layer or long sleeved top, then layer on sweaters, cardigans, or fleece for added insulation. A stylish yet warm winter coat is required, preferably one that is water resistant and long enough to protect from wind and rain. Classic colors such as navy, charcoal, and camel look great against the city's holiday lights, while deep reds, greens, and metallic accents can add a seasonal flair to your photos.

Accessories are both functional and aesthetically pleasing. Scarves, hats, and gloves keep you warm and allow you to incorporate festive colors or textures into your outfits. Cozy wool socks and comfortable boots with good traction are essential for walking on wet cobblestones, providing stability and comfort without sacrificing style. Boots in leather or suede finish photograph well and look great with both casual and dressier outfits.

For those planning evening outings or special events, such as light shows or Christmas concerts, adding elegant touches like statement jewelry, a chic beret, or a tailored coat can elevate your look while keeping you warm. Layered outfits provide flexibility: you can remove a sweater indoors while still looking polished for photos.

Practical considerations include carrying a small cross body bag or backpack for essentials and avoiding bulky items that may disrupt your silhouette in photographs. Choosing coordinated, seasonally inspired outfits allows for more cohesive photos throughout the city, from illuminated squares and Winter Wonders markets to cozy cafés and cobblestone streets.

By balancing comfort, warmth, and festive style, visitors can fully enjoy Brussels' holiday charm while taking beautiful, memorable photographs that capture the city's magic during the Christmas season.

Printed in Dunstable, United Kingdom